INDIAN RESPONSE
TO
AFRICAN WRITING

INDIAN RESPONSE TO AFRICAN WRITING

Edited by

A. Ramakrishna Rao
C.R. Visweswara Rao

P R E S T I G E

Published by
Prestige Books
3/28, East Patel Nagar,
New Delhi 110 008

ISBN: 81-85218-71-4

1993

Phototypesetting by
data culture
New Delhi 110 065
Ph. 6431070

Printed at
Mehra Offset Press
New Delhi 110 002

CONTENTS

Preface 9

1. The Politics of the Anglophone African Discourse
A. Ramakrishna Rao 13

2. Plinths against Unreason: Myth and Ritual in Wole Soyinka's Post-Biafran Writings
Mary T. David 21

3. Soyinka's Use of 'the Displaced Myth' in *Idanre*
M.S. Nagarajan 33

4. The Use of Cross-Cultural Myth in Soyinka's *The Bacche of Euripides*
K. Santhanam 41

5. J.P. Clark's *Ozidi* and African Theatre
N. Eakambaram 47

6. The African Voice: The Griot in Ayi Kwei Armah's *The Healers*
R.M.V. Raghavendra Rao 59

7. Okonkwo and His *Chi*
S. Krishna Sarma 66

8. Myth and Symbolism in the Novels of Chinua Achebe
S.A. Khayyoom 71

9. Pre- and Post-Colonial Society in Achebe's Novels
N. Rama Devi 79

10. Ngugi and the New Historiography
C.R. Visweswara Rao 87

11. Politicizing Language:
The Relevance of Ngugi's Rejection of English
S.V. Srinivas 98

12. Writers in Politics: Ngugi's *Detained* and
K V R's *Detenu Diary:* A Study
N. Somasekhara Sarma 105

13. The Writer's Conscience:
A Reading of Nadine Gordimer's *The Essential Gesture*
C. Subbarao 113

Index 119

For
Sri G.V. Rao

Notes on Contributors

Prof. Mary T. David is Professor of English at Mother Teresa University for Women, Madras.

Mrs. N. Rama Devi is Lecturer in English at S.K. University, Anantapur.

Dr. N. Eakambaram is Reader in English, University of Madras. Madras.

Dr. S.A. Khayyoom is Reader in English at S.K. University, Anantapur.

Prof. M.S. Nagarajan is Professor of English at the University of Madras, Madras.

Dr. R.M.V. Raghavendra Rao is Head of the Dept. of English at Bhavan's New Science, Arts and Commerce College, Hyderabad.

Prof. A. Ramakrishna Rao is Professor of English at S.K. University, Anantapur.

Dr. C.R. Visweswara Rao is Reader in English, S.K. University, Anantapur.

Dr. K. Santhanam is Lecturer in English, Jamal Mohamed College, Trichirapalli.

Prof. S. Krishna Sarma is Professor of English at Nagarjuna University, Guntur.

Sri N. Somasekhara Sarma is Lecturer in English at Government Degree College, Anantapur.

Sri S. V. Srinivas is Research Scholar in the Department of English at the University of Hyderabad, Hyderabad.

Prof. C. Subbarao is Professor of English at Dr. B.R. Ambedkar Open University, Hyderabad.

PREFACE

Any generalization about the Third World writing seems to be a hazardous venture in terms of contemporary critical theory. In assessing the value and significance of the twentieth-century African writing, the outsider has to be more careful because of the vast and varied linguistic landscape colonial and the post-colonial Africa presents. Mbella Sonne Dipok seems to suggest a perspective when he says:

> Let us as Africans
> Define an Afican sanctity
> A purity by which to live
> And die
> For the love of our people
> Who are asking to be led
> towards a better future.[1]

The ethnopoetic aspiration outlined in the preceding citation seems to be acceptable to most African writers. As Soyinka observes, "it is possible to claim that the lack of stylistic contrivance in modern African literature is due to the refusal of the artist to respond to the blandishments of literary ideology—manifesto art. Much African writing is still rooted in the concept of literature as a part of the normal social activity of man but which, nonetheless individual in its expression and its *choice* of areas of concern."[2] The crucial word in the preceding citation is "choice." Whether an African writer should choose to reflect in his writing the injustice and the victimization he faced in the hands of the rulers or should he take a polemic, if not a hostile, attitude to everything that is western can best be left to the writer himself. In this context the critic's job is to analyse the medium through which the writerly concerns are conveyed to the reader, native/foreign. In some quarters there remains the feeling that the non-white writers address their writing to the western readers. A careful study of these literatures seems to indicate the contrary. Achebe thinks that the new literature in Africa is aware of the possibilities available to it for celebrating humanity in our continent.[3] It is aware also that our world interlocks more and more with the worlds of others. Achebe seems to suggest the stock-in-trade idea of modern critical theory that no literature is insular in its origin and significance. Readers nourished on Conrad's *The Heart of Darkness* or Eliot's 'Tradition and the Individual Talent' or E.M. Forster's *A Passage to India* may require an adjustment of their perspectives to cope with the freshness, sometimes the erratic value, of writing which belongs to a tradition, a way and a view of life, which are unfamiliar.

II

The most controversial aspect of African writing appears to be the medium and an imaginative perspective and rhetoric derived from Eurocentric sensitivity. Most African writers opt for English, maybe to reach a wider audience. Since he is very much conscious that his choice deprives him of the linguistic resources of his own language for creative use, the writer tries to indigenize the medium. A theorist of African discourse observes, "as both a method and a decolonizing strategy, it attempts to convey the concepts, thought patterns and even linguistic features of the African language through the European tongue."[4] But as the theorist points out, these attempts have not succeeded and a future reader may get a doubt whether he is reading African Europhone or African language texts. Whatever the theoretical implications of this may be, writers like Ngugi are conscious of an ethnic betrayal when they use a foreign language to express the fate of the people. One way out of this impasse appears to be to practise auto-translation. The writer himself translates his work from his own language to the other. This seems to eliminate too much of foot-note or subtext that one often comes across in the African Europhone writing.

Keeping the foregoing perspectives about the African discourse in mind, if we turn to the papers presented at the seminar, we find that more than the issue of the medium, the emphasis at the seminar was on the message. Given the Indian context, this is not a complex matter and can be adequately explained. Indian writing in English has come of age. There have been a number of mature works which have received global acclaim. In spite of a multi-language society in our country, there has been an increasing awareness that English is one of the languages of the country capable of expressing views and adequate for all practical purposes. So the participants seem to be at home with African writing in English. It has to be admitted that the critical focus was on the established classics in African writing, Soyinka, Achebe, Ngugi, Clarke, and Gordimer. At this point we have also to consider the accessibility of texts. Given this restraint, it appears from a close perusal of the papers included in this volume that they show an awareness of the growing significance of the subject and a fresh interpretative response. The Editors are not offering this collection of essays as the apologists of African writing. The venture is a disinterested critical activity, and this is amply borne out by the papers.

The Editors express their grateful thanks to Prof. K. Venkata Reddy, Former Vice-Chancellor, Sri Krishnadevaraya University, for sanctioning the National Seminar on African literature at which the essays collected in this volume were presented. But for the patronage extended by Sri V.K. Srinivasan, I.A.S., Former Vice-Chancellor of the University, the conduct of the seminar looked impossible at one stage. The Editors owe a debt of gratitude to the Oriental Insurance Company Ltd., especially to its Chairman-cum-Managing Director,

Sri G.V. Rao. The Indian Society for Commonwealth Studies, New Delhi, and Prof. R.K. Dhawan, its Co-ordinating Secretary, deserve special mention for collaborating with us in the conduct of the National Seminar and for helping us bring out this volume of essays. The Editors are deeply thankful to the staff of the Department of English. Sri Krishnadevaraya University, for their co-operation and support. Students and Research Scholars, by their ready and prompt help, contributed their mite to the success of the seminar and the Editors thank them for it.

A.R.R.
C.R.V.

NOTES

1. Mbella Sonne Dipoko, *Black and White in Love* (London: Heinemann Educational Books, 1982), p. 49.
2. Wole Soyinka, *Myth, Literature and the African World* (Cambridge: Cambridge Univ. Press, 1979), pp. 66-67. Emphasis added.
3. Chinua Achebe, "African Literature as Restoration of Celebration," *Kunapipi:* Special Issue in Celebration of Chinua Achebe, XII, 2 (1990), p. 10.
4. Chantal Zabus, "Othering the Foreign Language in the West African Europhone Novel,' *Canadian Review of Comparative Literature*, XVII, Nos. 3 & 4, September/December 1990, p. 349.

The Politics of Anglo-Phone African Discourse

A. RAMAKRISHNA RAO

SATIE, AT THE END OF TERM

The mind's eye aches from Henry James,
Like arms from heavy cases, lugged for miles.
Theme and structure, imagery and tone.

From Lawrence, too: how hard I dug
For insights sunk, yards deep, in turgid prose.
Theme and structure, imagery and tone.

Web of necessity in *Daniel Deronda*,
Gloom in *Dorrit*, gloom in Flaubert,
One more week to go, at
Theme and structure, imagery and tone.

So, fitful-fresh as April Sun,
You're welcome, clown;
Your good melodic dissonance
will pierce low clouds of syllabus
with humour's grace,
Mercy of irreverence.

Simon Curtis[1]

Achebe's *Anthills of the Savannah* dramatizes the fortunes of three intelligent men who are fatally caught in the corridors of power. The novel is in a way a subtle and suggestive explication of the dynamics of power. The political turmoil in the state of Kangan is foregrounded in the legend of Idemili, the daughter of the Almighty, who sends her to the earth "to bear witness to the moral nature of authority by wrapping around power's nude waist a loincloth of peace and modesty."[2] She descends to the world as the resplendent pillar of water. But in the course of centuries the *Pillar of Water transforms* herself into "numberless shrine houses across the country, a dry stick rising erect from the bare, earth floor." (103) The narrator explains the transformation as follows: "Man's best artifice to share and hold the grandeur of divinity always crumbles in his hands, and the more ardently he strives, the more paltry and incongruous the result. So it were better he did not try at all; far better to ritualize that incongruity and by invoking the *mystery of metaphor* to hint at the most unattainable glory by its very opposite, the most mundane starkness—a mere stream, a tree, a stone, a mound of earth, little clay bowl containing fingers of chalk." (103, emphasis added) Achebe seems to think that the transformation of divinity into a ritualistic object is metaphoricity at its most suggestive plane. But his mythified metaphor thrives on ontological naivety. In the text we notice a demytholozing curve and a demystification of metaphor. Beatrice Nwanyibuife in her eagerness to heal the breach between Chris Orika, her lover, and Ikem Osodi, her poet-friend, plays the role of Idemili with marginal success. But what is to be emphasized here is that Beatrice, a top member of the country civil service, does not know her own roots. "So she came to barely knowing who she was. Barely, we say though, because she did carry a vague sense, more acute at certain critical moments than others of being *two different people*." (100, emphasis added) But Ikem is aware of this. In her he sees "the village priestess who will prophesy when her divinity rides her abandoning if need be her soup-pot on the fire, but returning again when the God departs to the domesticity of the kitchen." The expression "*two different people*" is an obvious reference to the Colonial complex which is further complicated by the "missionary mishmash." (105)

Beatrice is a sensitive character with a fine sensibility. She is not interested in the African birds and the sounds they make. But one morning a bird's voice compels her attention. The bird cries, "The Kings Property. . . . Is the Kings property correct." This is reminiscent of a similar story of a bird told by her mother. So she reflects that "two whole generations of the like of me could take a first class degree in English, there were already barely literate carpenters and artisans of British rule hacking away in the archetypical jungle and subverting the very sounds and legends of day break to make straight my way." (106) As an important member of the country's civil service, she is very much aware of the tension prevailing between traditional orthodoxy and the Eurocentric ideological invasion. But she seems to agree with Iken, the poet. "Do I contradict my self." asked Walt Whitman. "Very well, I contradict myself," he sang defiantly, "I am large, I contain multitudes." Every artist contains multitudes. Graham Greene is a Roman Catholic, a partisan of Rome if you like. Why then does he write so compulsively about bad, doubtful and doubting priests? Because a genuine artist, no matter what he says he believes, must feel in his blood the ultimate enmity between art and orthodoxy." (160)

II

Achebe's *Anthills of the Savannah* was published in 1987. A year before it was published, *Critical Inquiry* brought out a special number, "Race, Writing and Difference" in which there was an interesting discussion on the African discourse. But most contributors are cautious in their approach. One of the contributors, for example, says, "one barrier facing those of us in the humanities has been methodological. Under Saussurian hegemony, we have too easily become accustomed to thinking of meaning as constituted by systems of difference purely internal to our endlessly structured *langues*. Race, we all assume, is like other concepts constructed by metaphor and metonymy; it stands metonymically, for the Other: it bears the weight metaphorically of other kinds of difference."[3] At the root of the idea of colonial discourse we have the assumption of otherness. It is supposed to be characterized by orality, tradition, folk culture which are in a binary opposition to the written, modern, civilized and urban. The authors of *Towards the Decolonization of African Literature*[4] argue that the post-structuralist Euro-American theory of discourse has an imperialist design on the African writing which has a history, tradition, norms and forms of its own. They are resentful of the Euromodernism of Soyinka and the Marxist contraptions of Ngugi. But a few defend Soyinka. Comparing him with the Jacobean playwrights and Arnold, Adrian A. Roscoe has said that *Idanre* "provides convincing testimony to his ability to work within the traditional Ifa system."[5] Craig Tapping commenting on Soyinka's *Myth, Literature, and the African World* says, "Grounded in the oratory of his traditional culture, Soyinka ritually invokes Gods before commencing on the most unoral of pursuits, comparative literary criticism."[6] Suggestive as the preceding observation is, it gives another twist to the African discourse by roping in the comparative poetics.

III

In the light of the creative perspective that emerges from Achebe's text, the foregoing observations seem to suffer from academic politics that is the hallmark of all critical enterprise. In our eagerness to participate in the politics of international critical theory, we sometimes refuse to take seriously what the artists say about their art. A brief review of the politics of Gods in Anglo-phone African Novel may dispel a few misconceptions about the African discourse.

In T. Obinkaram Echewa's *The Land's Lord* one of the village elders says, "All Gods are a little mad. If you have a mind to serve them properly, you should be a little drunk yourself."[7] The preceding statement is reminiscent of the words of the

Bastard, in *King John*: "Mad World! Mad Kings! Mad composition."[8] In T.M. Aluko's *One Man, One Wife*, a young villager, after a chequered career, turns into a prophet and says, "I open my eyes and see into the years to come. I see people casting their idols into flames. I see the Lord, Jehovah Himself, feeding the flames with oil from a jar that he holds in his hands. I see the dolls go up in smoke—Shonponna, the God of small pox, of Ogun, the God of iron, of Shango, the God of thunder and lightning, and of Orisaoko, the Goddess of Harvest." In Achebe's *Arrow of God* the narrator says, "the festival thus brought Gods and men together in one crowd. It was the only assembly in Umuaro in which a man might look to his right and find his neighbour and look to his left and see a God standing there—perhaps Agwu whose mother also gave birth to madness or Ngene, owner of a Stream."[10] But the curious thing about these novels is the divine betrayal. In the *Land's Lord*, Father Highler fails to save his pot-boiler, Philip, from the wrath of his clan. In *One Man, One Wife* Joshua, a respectable member of Isolo village, was struck down by lightning. His accidental death is interpreted as the wrath of Shango, the God of lightning, whom Joshua does not displease. In fact, he is more loyal to Shango than to the God of Christianity. Ezeulu, in *Arrow of God*, is let down by his God Ulu in his struggle against the clan. Ezeulu's fate is explained by the poęple of Umuaro very briefly: "Their God had taken sides with them against his headstrong and ambitious priest and thus upheld the wisdom of their ancestors—that no man however great was greater than his people; that no man ever won judgment against his clan."[11]

A point that is to be noted in assessing these novels is the tension generated by the presence of the native Gods and Christ. In other words, the coexistence of mass, catechism and choir practice and sacrifice and ritual. As the narrator of *The Land's Lord* observes, "The villagers the christian and non-christian doted on ceremonies."[12]

IV

From the foregoing commentary one point seems to be clear enough. Because of the missionary activity the African has developed the capacity to question the premises of his mythical world. The mystery of metaphor seems to have lost its mystification so that an artist could use it as a trope to control the rhetoricity of his discourse. But he is not unaware of what he does and is doing. No doubt, there are contradictions in his construing and reconstructing the past. But as Achebe's Ikem rightly observes, "contradictions if well understood and managed can spark off fires of invention. Orthodoxy, whether of the right or of the left is the graveyard of creativity."(100) Every African writer is "two people." He is born to a worldview which is mytheopic, ritualistic, hierarchical, authoritarian, folk-oriented, oral and tribal. But by a historical accident he has become aware of a culture that is rational, actuality-oriented, techno-scientific, pragmatic and endowed with an established discourse. As an artist he has to evolve a discourse and its enunciative modalities which are inclusive and viable to meet his creative challenge. The given tradition, its past and present relevance, its juxtaposition with the alien tradition have to find a place. But much of it is available in terms of mythified metaphor, which needs to be given a meaning. Meaning emerges the moment it is demystified and finds a place in the rhetoricity of the discourse. Normally a metaphor acts in two ways. It makes the unfamiliar familiar and expands the familiar so as to make it unfamiliar. In this way it crystallizes the hermeneutic core of the discourse. The texts I have cited and analysed do not exclude the contradictions but accommodate them in the discourse.

Most critics of the third-world literature may often think that a third world artist often writes for Anglo-American or European audience. This is a false notion. For example, *Things Fall Apart* had better sales in Nigeria than in the U.S.A. or the U.K. or Europe. A writer is the most sensitive point of his community. It is not significant to note that a particular writer is influenced by a particular image of life, or a world view or a theory of discourse. But it is significant to note that his discourse interprets the consciousness of his people.

Soyinka seems to have had this in mind when he christened his novel, *The Interpreters*. The much talked of African oral tradition does not by itself provide a readymade discourse to the artist. When the tradition is demystified and the artist is capable of making the demystified metaphor an inseparable part of the discourse, he has the power to interpret the past in the light of the present. Not only the African discourse but any discourse written in a foreign language is interpretative in this sense, and has within itself the hermeneutic system, with the help of which a reader can make it explicit.

NOTES

1. Kingsley Amis, ed., *The Oxford Book of Light Verse* (London: OUP, 1978), pp. 328-29.
2. This and all other citations are from Achebe, *The Anthills of the Savannah* (London: Picador Books, 1988), p. 102.
3. Anthony Appiah, "The Uncompleted Argument," *Critical Inquiry*, Vol. 12, No. 1, 1985, p. 35.
4. Onwwchekwa Jemie Chinweizeu and Ihechuckwu Madwbuike, *The Decolonisation of African Literature*, Vol. 1 (Washington: Howard University Press, 1983).
5. Adrian Roscoe, "Soyinka as Poet" in William Walsh, ed., *Readings in Commonwealth Literature* (Oxford: Clarenden Press, 1970), p. 280.
6. Craig Tapping, "Voices off, Models of Orality in African Literature and Literary Criticism," *Ariel*, Vol. 21, No. 3, July 1990, p. 83.
7. T. Obinkaram Echewa, *The Land's Lord* (London: Heineman Educational Books, 1976), p. 1.
8. Peter Alexander, ed., *William Shakespeare: The Complete Works* (London: Collins, rpt. 1960), p. 424.
9. T.M. Aluko, *One Man, One Wife* (London: Heinemann Educa-

tional Books, rep. 1980), p. 147.
10. Chinua Achebe, *Arrow of God* (London: Heinemann Educational Books, 1964), p. 254.
11. *Ibid.*, p. 287.
12. *Land's Lord*, p. 64.

"Plinths . . . against Unreason"—
Myth and Ritual in
Soyinka's Post-Biafran Writings

MARY T. DAVID

The first five years following Soyinka's release from detention in 1969 saw the publication, in quick succession, of five of his important works—*Madmen and Specialists* (1971), *The Man Died* and *A Shuttle in the Crypt* (1972), *The Bacchae of Euripides* (1973) and *Season of Anomy* (1974). These were all conceived in prison, and scribbled, as the author tells us between the pages of Paul Radin's *Primitive Religion* and his own *Idanre.*[1] Their composition took place under constant threat to his life and the ever-present fear that measures were being taken "both to contain and destroy his mind."[2] In his note to *The Man Died* Soyinka testifies to the fact that the mind in solitary confinement traverses strange and sinister by-ways and begets strange monsters. How, we are apt to ask, did his own mind escape this fate and survive intact the "shock-disorientation techniques" of the "mind-butchers"? His will-power was enormous, but the answer is also to be found in a certain quality that all these works have in common, namely, a great reliance on mythic references, images and symbols. His mythopoesis and ritualization of experience helped him to grapple with the chaos and turmoil and give some order and significance to them. Soyinka has from the beginning of his literary career made use of myth and ritual, but during the two years' solitary confinement they sustained and safeguarded him against the madness that raged around him and threatened to overwhelm him. They were indeed, to borrow a phrase of his from *A Shuttle in the Crypt*, "plinths . . . against unreason."[3]

The myths that absorb his interest in these works centre on the theme of regeneration and healing—a theme that assumed desperate urgency in the context of a protracted war and all its horrors. And the myths are used not only in the creative works but even in the prison notes. The orphic myth of descent into Hades, which Soyinka used in a readily recognizable form in the novel *Season of Anomy* is first used in a subdued way in *The Man Died.* The book begins with the author's entrance into the prison, which is identified with Hell. Dante's line "abandon hope all who enter here" suggests itself to his mind as he stands in front of his cell. Throughout the book prison is referred to as a burial place, vault, crypt and the metaphoric identification with Hell is sustained by references to the prison functionaries as 'Pluto,' and "The horned devil that came in with swishing forked tail and stamping hooves."[4] The prisoner feels the need "to control the debris of memory in the Waters of Lethe"[5] and when a child is born in an adjoining cell he feels that it should be christened Persephone. The pattern is complete when the book concludes though not with actual release yet with strong intimations of freedom. The prisoner is taken out and led to hospital and the experience is described as "the first unwrapping of the mummy."[6] The emergence from death to life is marked by the life-renewing rain. "Soaked to the skin, lashed by wind and rain, as we fled through the long unprotected corridors of the hospital I was struck suddenly by the phenomena of this wild, free yet governed motion of the elements and us and its contrast with that first death march into an artificial tomb."[7] It was as though cosmic confirmation was being given to the victory of the ineluctable forces of love and the unfettered principle of life. Thus the conclusion is laden with mythic motifs—of the ascent from Hell, of rebirth marked by the ritual of baptism and of the eternal conflict between the forces of death and evil and those of life and love. This emergence into life, this renewal, is foreshadowed in the book by a reference to Cocteau's *Orphee Negre* and its symbol of the dance of spring by two children "heirs to the evocative magic of sunrise, of seed awakening in the soil, beneath their tread of innocence."[8] "Children's voices in the orient" or heard in the leaves becomes a favourite auditory image that Soyinka uses in this phase where it has definite relevance to the theme of regeneration, as it has in Eliot's *The Waste Land* and *The Four Quartets.*

The Orphic myth is more transparently used by Soyinka in his novel *Season of Anomy.* 'Ofeyi' and 'Iriyise' are names that come very close to Orpheus and Eurydice. Ofeyi embarks on a quest for his lost Iriyise, and the quest takes him right into Temoko, the centre of the inferno. Soyinka builds up the mythic parallel by the depiction of the horrors and the detail of the human 'watch-dog' guarding the yard of the lunatics in which Iriyise is hidden. This human equivalent of 'Cerberus' is given the name Suberu,—an interesting fact when we remember that in Indian mythology the animal that guards the entrance to the underworld is *Sabera.* Soyinka was not unacquainted with Indian mythology and the presence of a strong Indian element in the story argues in favour of the view that 'Suberu' is a deliberate echo of *Sabera.*

However, the most important concern of the novel is regeneration and healing, and the quest for this is made to blend with the quest for Iriyise whom Soyinka identifies with Persephone and the quickening of Nature's life. "Her fingers spliced wounded saplings with the ease of a natural healer. Her presence, the women boasted inspired the rains."[9] The chapter titles of the novel—Seminal, Buds, Tentacles, Harvest, Spores,—show how closely the novel is structured on the rhythms of Nature which in Soyinka's works always embody the message of renewal. The community of Aiyero rests solidly on these rhythms of Nature. They "acknowledge their debts to the earth and the sea"[10] and their leader bears the designation "Custodian of the Grain." And 'grain' we are reminded means not merely food but germination. It is Ofeyi's aim to bring the life-giving, life-sustaining potencies of Aiyero to the waste land dominated by the Cartel, and its healing essence to "the festering continent." Standing by the "well of Restoration" at Aiyero, Ofeyi muses on the momentous nature of the task. Addressing the invisible denizens of that space he asks:

> What answers shall I make you then, you restless questioners rising from dank silt-beds. How change your whitened bones into something rich and strange? The lines had haunted him from his first glimpse of the pristine moment—full fathom five his father lies . . . of his bones are coral made . . . those are pearls. . . .[11]

Soyinka, we notice, uses the song of Ariel as a transformation symbol very much as Eliot has used it in *The Waste Land.* When a little later we find Ofeyi muttering: "Camouflage! The regenerative powers were only jealously contained within the pool hidden but attainable, awaiting only the rightful challenger,"[12] we see a little more distinctly the novel's closeness to the Waste Land myth. According to the myth, regeneration of the land and the healing of the King were possible and were meant to be, but the right Challenger had to come, the Quester. Ofeyi sees himself in this role and later in the novel we are told that he has the hands of the healer. Though the regeneration of the waste land is not actually shown as taking place in the novel, there is a hint of a promise in the concluding sentence: "In the forests life began to stir."[13]

The reason for Aiyero's being urged as a viable alternative to tyranny is its closeness to the earth, and the consequent spiritual richness. It rests on the truth stated by Eliot that "the natural life and the supernatural have a conformity to each other which neither has with the mechanistic life."[14] To Soyinka being earthed is the most important mode of being and his reiterated preference to be close to the earth is the result of his belief in nature's "life-sustaining draughts." *Madmen and Specialists* and Soyinka's adaptation of *The Bacchae* are dramatic statements of his conviction of Earth's sanctity and of what he calls "earth's regenerate need." *Madmen and Specialists* has been generally held up as an expression of Soyinka's pessimism and cynicism in the face of the atrocities of the war. Amid charges of denseness and lack of meaning what has gone unnoticed is the Yoruba belief implicit in the play—that Onile, the Earth goddess "is polluted by the shedding of blood except in Sacrifice and demands costly rites of purification and atonement."[15] Unlike the supreme god, Olorun Olodumare, this goddess has a cult because she interacts directly with mankind. This cult is the Ogboni cult, references to which appear in several of Soyinka's works. These references and the fact that the Ogboni cult was strongest in Abeokuta, from where Soyinka hails, point to the fact that the dramatist was not unaware of the belief in Onile. A bit of the dialogue from *Madmen and Specialists* can be illuminating here. The context is Bero's sudden arrival from the war to a joyous welcome from his sister. Si Bero pours libation on the earth and insists on removing the shoes from his feet.

> Bero: You still keep up these little habits?
> Si Bero: I like to keep close to earth.
> Bero (stepping back to prevent her from taking off his boots.): Bare feet, wet earth. *We've wetted your good earth with something more potent than that, you know.*[16] (My emphasis)

So at the centre of the play lies this sacrilege to the earth and the whole tragedy is to be viewed as the grim consequence of the violation of this taboo and the defiant boasting of it. Earth demands expiation and thus we have the play's denouement where two powerful strands of ritural purification converge. One of these is purification through fire, performed by the old women, Iya Agba and Iya Mate, who are not witches but the externalization of the healing essences of the earth. That they are to be equated with the earth is clear from their words: "We move as the Earth moves, we age as Earth ages."[17] In reply to Bero's threat to proscribe them, they ask, "What can that mean? You'll proscribe Earth itself?"[18] Their watchful presence in the play culminates in the ritual cleansing through fire. In answer to Si Bero's plea "And the good that is here? Does that count for nothing?" Iya Agba replies, "We'll put that into the test. Let us see how it takes to fire."[19] Fire appears in Soyinka's works as a purifying symbol, sometimes in metaphors of alchemy and metallurgy. But in *Anomy* and *Shuttle* Soyinka speaks of "fire that heals." So the embers hurled by the Earth Mothers are not meant as effecting destruction, but purification. It is certainly a ritual of cleansing which synchronizes with the other rite of expiation in the play—the sacrifice of Old Man. Bero's murder of his father, the severing of his last link with humanity, has, however, definite ritualistic overtones. It is a sacrificial death, for in this strange old man are conflated many roles. His likeness to Socrates is hinted at by Bero and it is strengthened by his death. He is a healer by profession and when he says "A part of me identifies with every human being,"[20] the remark establishes his identification with the Saviour who is also a Scapegoat and his death assumes the nature of a sacrifice. When Soyinka wrote *A Dance of the Forest* he was free with words like 'regeneration' and 'expiation,' but at the time of writing *Madmen and Specialists,* he felt the atmosphere of evil so dense and so near that he could not use the words but had to show the atonement being acted out for the crime of the Earth's pollution.

Soyinka's adaptation of *The Bacchae* brings into focus his belief that the earth has to be renewed through sacrifice, an idea that Eliot presents from the reference point of Christianity:

> War among men defiles the world
> But death in the Lord renews it.[21]

The idea of martyrdom haunts Soyinka and he believes that "the earth's regenerate need" is met by sacrificial blood. This is the thrust of his adaptation of the Greek play and is expressed by Tiresias:

> Perhaps . . . our life-sustaining earth
> Demands . . . a little more . . .
> Sometimes a more
> Than token offering for her own needful renewal.[22]

This is why the threnody of Euripides is turned into a communion rite, and Dionysus assumes a very close likeness to Ogun who is described by Soyinka as "elder brother to Dionysus."[23] He is "Restorer of fullness to Nature's lean hours."[24] Dionysus is "the rustle of wind in pine forests, shaking winter into life, with green branches," and his wine is "the sun that comes after winter, the power that nudges earth awake."[25] At the centre of *The Bacchae of Euripides* lies the idea of regeneration. The theogony of Dionysus and the renewal of Thebes coincide with the annual Elusinean festival. Tiresias who acts as a 'carrier' of the evils of the dying year confesses to a longing to taste the ecstasy of rejuvenation after long organizing its ritual. This rejuvenation is effected by Dionysus the god-head manifest in all Nature's vitality and renewal, the divine essence that is sweeping in its revolutionary force. Pentheus foolishly resists that force but unwittingly works for its fulfilment in his role as the sacrifice. The focus of Soyinka's play is the sacrificial death of Pentheus which is the central point in the Orphic adaptation of the Dionysian myth. Soyinka makes this point clear in terms that recall Frazer's Kings when he makes Dionysus explain to Pentheus:

> Yes, you alone
> Make sacrifice for your people, you alone.
> The role belongs to a King. Like the gods who yearly
> Must be rent to spring anew, that also
> is the future of heroes.[26]

Thus Pentheus who resists Dionysus the new god ends up as the sacrifice to the god and in that role of sacrifice becomes identified with the god—becomes a surrogate god. And so the wine spouting from the orifices of Pentheus' head becomes the blood of the god. A communion rite is thus shared, a mystic partaking of the blood of the deity.

Soyinka's interest in sacrifice as a theme goes back to his early works and can be traced to the Yoruba beliefs in the efficacy of *Ebo, Etutu* or propitiatory sacrifice "in purifying individuals and the community."[27] His imagination loves to linger over sacrificial rites and an early evidence of this comes in the highly evocative language in *The Interpreters* laying the setting for Sekoni's death on the road which has sacrificial overtones:

> The rains of May become in July still arteries of the Sacrificial bull, a million bleeding punctures of the sky bull hidden in convulsive cloud humps. . . . The blood of earth-dwellers mingles with blanched streams of the mocking bull, and flows into currents eternally below earth.[28]

What is evoked here is actualized in *Anomy* where Soyinka devotes several pages to describe the bull sacrifice at Aiyero performed by Pa Ahime.

> His knife-hand moved once—slashed deep and drew across the throat. The taut skin parted easily, opening to a layer of translucent membrane, yielding in turn to tendons and a commencement of red mists. . . . Ahime stepped back quickly. . . . His white vestments bloomed suddenly with small red petals and a long sigh rose, fell and filled the air with whispers of wind and the opening of buds. He moved swiftly now . . . a thousand eyes followed the motions of the priest whose flutist blade was laid again and again to ivory pipes, tuned to invocations of renewal.[29]

We also notice a very artful extension of the role of the sacrifice to Iriyise who, though spectator, is soon to be the sacrificial victim. This identification is managed purely through imagery.

> Iriyise beside him, a distant stillness. Her ivory neck piece had merged with hidden rapids in the bull's convulsive throats. Caryatid and timeless, only the warmth of her finger reassured him of her living flesh, a willing presence at the altar.[30]

In *The Man Died* and *Shuttle* we find Soyinka turning over the idea of sacrifice and trying to relate it to the blood-shed that was rocking the very foundation of his nation. The deaths of Okigbo and Victor Banjo are viewed as "burnt offerings," but Soyinka rejects the temptation to regard the massacre as a necessary ritual of renewal. The temptation certainly came to his mind in the persuasive reasoning:

> Yet blood must flow, a living flood
> Bravely guarded, boldly split
> A potency to rejuvenate
> Mothers-of-all earth . . .[31]

But this is rejected as "stale deception" and "Blasphemer's consolation." For

> This was death in evil, death without hue
> This death wore the cloak of scavengers.[32]

The Eucharist is a significant symbol in all that Soyinka has written. It is not merely the central rite of Christianity but the major ritual of the Mystery Religions which emphasized the idea of a new birth. In *A Shuttle* Soyinka makes repeated use of this ritual referring to it as communion, love-feast, Last Supper etc., and the image of the cup or the Missal or the Grail runs through this volume. When evil seems to triumph and all spiritual values are gone the poet can best express that condition as a travesty and corrupting of this and other sacred rites and symbols. Thus we hear of "fouled Communion" and "Earth's rites of defilement."

"Wailing Wall" lists a series of sacramental symbols as tainted or perverted— "tattered surplice," "broken Word," "altars of evil." Evil we are told "is impenitent and feeds upon the wounds and fears of pity" and hope is "buried in soil of darkness."[33]

Yet hope struggles all through *A Shuttle* and breaks out in lovely images of cleansing and purifying and renewal—images of "flesh being nibbled clean," of "voices of rain in sunshine," of spring-rites and seedling hands and of children's voices at the door of the orient. Hope of renewal is timid and tremulous.

> I do not
> Dare to think these bones will bloom tomorrow.[34]

But the provenance of the image which is the book of Ezekiel would seem to indicate that hope is viable. The mood and tone and images with which *A Shuttle in the Crypt* concludes also definitely indicate that the poet has wrestled with despair and learned to fix his gaze on the promise of restitution and healing. The last poems celebrate the sacrifice of Okigbo and Victor Banjo and others who

> Set upon the quest
> Seeking that whose plenitude
> Would answer calls of hate and terror,[35]

and who died as "burnt offering on the heights."[36]

During the intensely felt experiences of the war and his own imprisonment Soyinka's mythopoeic sensibility is reflected more insistently in his works than in an earlier or later period when the writer's penchant for satire has had brilliant display. The creative period prior to Biafra is marked by the hilarious comedy *Lion and the Jewel* and the sunny satire of Brother Jero. After the period under discussion Soyinka turned once again to satire as in *Opera Wonyosi,*[37] *Requiem for a Futurologist* and his recent *A Play of the Giants.* But under the searing experiences of the war and incarceration, myth and ritual afforded him not only inspiration but also, in R. Frost's phrase, "a stay against confusion."

NOTES

1. Wole Soyinka, *The Man Died* (Penguin Books, 1977), p. 9.
2. *Ibid.*
3. Wole Soyinka, *A Shuttle in the Crypt* (London: Rex Collings/ Eyre Methuen, 1972), p. 3.
4. Wole Soyinka, *The Man Died*, p. 242.
5. *Ibid.*, p. 132.
6. *Ibid.*, p. 288.
7. *Ibid.*, p. 290.
8. *Ibid.*, pp. 198-99.
9. Wole Soyinka, *Season of Anomy* (London: Rex Collings), p. 20.
10. *Ibid.*, p. 10.
11. *Ibid.*, p. 90.
12. *Ibid.*, p. 91.
13. *Ibid.*, p. 320.
14. T.S. Eliot, *The Idea of a Christian Society* (London: Faber & Faber, 1939), p. 61.
15. Norton Williams, "African Beliefs and Religions" in *Peoples and Cultures of Africa*, ed. Eliott P. Skinner (N.Y., 1973).
16. Wole Soyinka, *Madmen and Specialists* in *Wole Soyinka: Collected Plays*, 2 (Oxford Paperbacks), p. 234.
17. *Ibid.*, p. 259.
18. *Ibid.*, p. 260.
19. *Ibid.*, p. 274.
20. *Ibid.*, p. 264.
21. T.S. Eliot, *Murder in the Cathedral* in *Complete Poems and Plays of T.S. Eliot* (Faber and Faber), p. 263.
22. Wole Soyinka, *The Bacchae of Euripides*, in *Wole Soyinka: Collected Plays*, p. 306.
23. *Ibid.*, p. 234.
24. *Ibid.*, p. 250.
25. *Ibid.*, p. 259.
26. *Ibid.*, p. 293.

27. J.O. Awolalu, *Yoruba Beliefs and Sacrificial Rites* (London: Longman, 1979), p. 152.
28. Wole Soyinka, *The Interpreters*, p. 155.
29. Wole Soyinka, *Season of Anomy*, p. 16.
30. *Loc. cit.*
31. Wole Soyinka, *A Shuttle in the Crypt*, p. 11.
32. *Ibid.*, p. 12.
33. *Ibid.*, p. 35.
34. *Ibid.*, p. 62. See also, Ezekiel 37: 2.
35. *Ibid.*, p. 88.
36. *Ibid.*, p. 89.
37. The satire is amply brought out by the title which in Yoruba means "The fool buys Wonyosi"—Wonyosi being an extravagantly expensive lace that was the rage among Nigerians till the government had to ban it.

Soyinka's Use of 'the Displaced Myth' in *Idanre*

M.S. NAGARAJAN

It is said that Wole Soyinka "operates completely within the English tradition." There seems to be a considerable degree of truth in such a statement; Soyinka's poetry has inescapable affiliations with Shakespeare, the Romantics and Dylan Thomas so far as mythic imagination goes. It is not impossible to choose passages from Soyinka and subject them to favourable comparisons with these English poets. But the truth is that he consciously breaks away from what he calls "the universal-humanoid abstraction" of the West which, for him, is obscurantist for it rationalizes or intellectualises myths and thereby impoverishes them. The Western philosophic systems of the nineteenth century have destroyed the concept of the dream, magic and mystery associated with myths. He argues, with conviction, in his *Myth, Literature and the African World* why creative works in Africa should be brought closer to myths. He is as clear about the use of the myth as he is about the rejection of negritude. Myth, for Soyinka, even as it is for Vico or Chase is a "blaze of reality." While the mythopoeic mode of presenting reality is fast losing ground in the Western world, in African poetry it has found its secure stay. Primitive thought is mythical whereas 'civilised' thought is matter-of-fact. Soyinka revivifies ancient African myths and uses them as disinherited, or better still, 'displaced' myths in his poetry. This paper attempts to examine his use of the displaced myth in his earliest poem *Idanre*, composed in 1965.

The more complex the myth of a nation, the richer the culture of its people. For Soyinka, the Yoruba cosmology is embodied in *Ifa*, the traditional religious belief of his countrymen. According to this system, Ogun is the first-born of Odudwa who founded the Yoruba race. There are several episodes connected with Ogun's exploits and the climax is that in which he is enraged at the sight of his countrymen celebrating the *Oriki* festival, without his knowledge. He comes down on them, killing them. When he drinks the palm-wine, he regains his senses and realises his folly. He kills himself, becomes a God and vows to his people that he will appear in the world to protect his kinsmen whenever they pray for his help. And from then on annual festivals are held when people visit his sacred shrine and appeal to his aid and protection for their well-being. Ogun, the man, was metamorphosed into a God and during festivals, when he is invoked, he appears in the form of an anthropomorphic *avatar*. This dual existence, the God-human form of Ogun, explains his paradoxical and contradictory nature. He is at once the destroyer and the preserver, the God of death and the God of life. Ogun is the God of Harvest; hence the farmers celebrate the harvest festival with sacrificial offerings to him.

Idanre has epic dimensions about it and the poem opens with the descent of Ogun into this world.

> Ogun is still on such
> Combatant angles, poised to a fresh descent
> Fiery axe-heads fly about his feet.

This long poem in four hundred and thirtyfive lines, using an uncommon stanzaic form of five lines seems to have been composed with "unpremeditated ease" during the course of an evening. In Section VI of the poem, Soyinka uses the term "Mobis Strip," which he explains as a "mathe-magical ring, infinite in self-recreation into independent but linked rings and therefore the freest conceivable (to me) symbol of human or divine (Yoruba Olympian) relationships." The poem also has the form of rings one within the other, interlinked, yet independent. Time past and time future are presented in time present. The first "segment" is "deluge . . ." and the last is "harvest." The movement thus is logical and natural but the intervening five sections take us through time and space presented through multiple consciousness and varied levels of perception and reality. The second section ". . . and after" transports us to

> . . . counterpane of nights since innocence
> Of apocalyptic skies, when thunderous shields clashed
> Across the heights. . . .

The third section "Pilgrimage" is a description of the journey of the protagonist with Ogun. The next segment, "the beginning" shows the fulfilment of Ogun's promise in recreating the world and the imagery employed in this section is that of a blacksmith casting and forging a new shape out of metals. Ogun is at once "a demanding God," and "a lascivious God." He would never allow "a mere plague of infinite chaos/ Stand between the gods and man."

> He made a mesh of elements, from stone
> Of fire in earthfruit, the womb of energies
> He made an anvil of the peaks, and kneaded
> Red clay for his mould.

Ogun forged a unity by defeating the existing deities, Orisanla, Orunnila, Esu, Ifa and was crowned the king by the elders of Ire. Segment V of the Sequence, "the battle" dramatises Ogun's day of error when he is on a wild rampage, destroying everyone, heedless of the cries of his own people.

> Storms strain his mighty chest, his nipples
> Glow with blackness, from hair-roots

Spit black jets of flames. Tall he rises to the hills
His head a rain-cloud has eclipsed the sun
His nostrils blow visible
Exhalations . . .

The devastation is complete; but when truth dawned upon the men of Ire, it was too late.

Too late came warning that a god
Is still a god to men, and men are one
When knowledge comes, of death.

In the penultimate segment "recessional," the protagonist arrives at an understanding of the mystery of life and death, after witnessing the spectacle of disaster, at the end of his journey with Ogun. The cyclical pattern of life and death is grasped by him. After all, the action of Atooda in unrolling the boulder down the hill is not just an accident; but is replete with meaning. Atooda's act is not one of treachery. He is the first revolutionary and is, therefore, raised to the heights of a saint, a saviour of society through an act of individual will. In the final section "harvest," Ogun departs, having disclosed his secrets to the protagonist. It is now left for him to reap the fruits of the real harvest, having gained an awareness of life's mysteries. We are brought back to the world of physical presences when the poet and the wine-girl who has been waiting for him all along, go on their way, from the forest to the world.

And they moved towards resorption in His alloy essence
Primed to a fusion, primed to the sun's dispersion
Containment and communion, seed-time and harvest, palm
And pylon, Ogun's road a 'Moribus' orbit, kernel
And electrons, wine to alchemy.

I have just attempted to give you a literal reading of the poem, or better still, a reworking of the story of Ogun in the form of a long poem. Northrop Frye, in his *Fables of Identity*, explaining the act of indirect mythologising in literature, uses the term "displacement." What he means by it is "putting works of literature in such a context so as to give them an immense reverberating dimension of significance. "In this reverberating significance "every literary work catches the echoes of all other works of its type in literature, and so ripples out into the rest of literature and thence into life. . . ." *Idanre* has the same structure as the mythology of Ogun and it is not an interpretation of its meaning. In "displacement," the relationship between the work of literature and mythology it presents is not allegorical. There is a direct experience of the mythology and hence it has its working power. The unifying shape of the whole design becomes visible conceptually. Aristotle refers to this process calling it *anagnorisis* which is often inadequately translated as "discovery" or "recognition." When a mythological system loses contact with people, it remains a mere allusion. This is sadly what has happened to Greco-Roman mythologies in Christian Europe. In such a situation, analogy and identity, so necessary for the moving power of a work, get blurred and then totally lost in course of time.

Soyinka employs the mythopoeic mode in order to convey certain deep concerns of humanity in the form of an appropriate vision. There is an inherent dynamism, a primitive vitality about his mythopoeic utterance, as in the African context mythologies are a system of shared beliefs. *Idanre* partakes of the nature of poetry as revelation of Soyinka's view of the world. What is this world view and how far is it valuable and significant for us? Soyinka seems to convey the idea that there is an endless, relentless, inescapable pattern of life and death for man. He seems to be condemned to fall a victim to this ill-fated cycle of infernal doom from which there is no deliverance. Salvation is possible, in some measure, through his own voluntary action, through his individual Will. Atooda is the slave of God; yet it was he who rolled down a piece of rock on his unsuspecting master, smashing him to bits and creating in the process, multiple godhead.

Man's passage, pre-ordained, self-ordered winds
In reconstruction.

Authority, even the sanctioned one, has to be subjected to constant questioning or resistance, if man has to break his shackles and survive in this world. Revolution, rather than slavish compliance, seems the solution.

Rather we may celebrate the stray electron, defiant
Of patterns, celebrate the splitting of the gods
Canonisation of the strong hand of a slave who set
The rock in revolution—and the Boulder cannot
Up the hill in time's unwind.

He shall teach us to ignite our several kilns
And glory in each bronzed emergence.

Human nature does not bear much scrutiny. There is no saving grace for man from above; search for guidance from moral or spiritual source is futile. Belief in some supervening act of a merciful God leads us nowhere. The only option left for man in such a grim situation is to rely on his individual Will and dare and act. The only escape from fatalism and determinism that envelop him is through action, positive action. Liberation is possible only through action. The leitmotif of *Idanre* is the quest for wisdom. The protagonist of the poem is presented as a diviner who, at the end of the journey, has a greater understanding and a deeper awareness of life. The concluding lines of the poem are pointers that there has been a growth in the protagonist's perception of the world. He is wiser for the journey. He becomes conscious of the enigma of the human situation, so full of contradictions, irrationalities.

Idanre does not exist at the level of mere description or narration of episodes. There is a ritual enactment of the whole mythical drama. The battle, the unleashing of weaponry of "lust-blind God" Ogun is real (as in a play) and even the wine-girl is perceived as a real being, living, out there on the roadside. Soyinka recreates Ogun in the modern world as "the God of Iron and metallurgy, Explorer, Artisan, Hunter, God of War, Guardian of the Road, the Creative Essence." Displacement of the mythical Gods demands a specialised vocabulary. Pastoral images will be out of place. And so the poem abounds in such scientific vocabulary as "electron," "atomised," "filaments," "protoplasmic," and "teguments."

Soyinka has more than his share of hostile critics. Many of his poems, for Roderick Wilson, "exhibit an inadequate working out of images and metaphors, slightness of theme and insufficiently full presentation of the theme or experience involved." (101) Ken Goodwin finds his poems "overloaded with possibilities and deficient in clear statement." (114) James Booth maintains that his poetry is "metaphorically irresponsible and syntactically messy." (70) These critical assessments have a great deal of truth in them and one finds it hard to refute them. It is possible to demonstrate, using the known criteria of applied criticism that there is a woeful lack of cohesion in Soyinka's language and thought, imprecision in his imagery, etc. But as a complex yet unified vision of the condition of man in the present-day world and the choices open to him, the poem remains wholly successful. And that depends, in no small measure, on Soyinka's displacement of the Yoruba Ogun myth in *Idanre* to suit our context. In his preface to the poem, he says, "In detail, in the human context of my society, *Idanre* has made abundant sense." A critic of Soyinka, D.I. Nwoga is of the view that his success in his coordination of poetic style, material content and significance "proceed convincingly from an imaginative perception of reality incorporating the mythical, human and natural worlds, a vision emanating from a vigorous, revolutionary spirit that will not yield to the oppressive conventions of fate and human wilfulness." (185) And that, precisely, is *Idanre* !

WORKS CITED

James Booth, "Myth, Metaphor and Syntax in Soyinka's Poetry," *Research in African Literature*, 17.1 (1986): 70.

Northrop Frye, *Fables of Identity: Studies in Poetic Mythology*. New York, 1963.

Ken Goodwin, *Understanding African Poetry: A Study of Ten Poets*. London: Heinemann, 1982. 114.

D.I Nwoga, "Poetry as Revelation: Wole Soyinka," *Critical Perspectives on Wole Soyinka*. Ed. James Gibbs. London: Heinemann, 1981.

Wole Soyinka, *Myth, Literature and the African World*. Cambridge: Cambridge UP, 1976.

——, *Idanre*. Methuen: London, 1967 (All references are to this edition of the text).

Roderick Wilson, "Complexity and Confusion in Soyinka's Shorter Poems," *Critical Perspectives on Wole Soyinka*. Ed. James Gibbs. London: Heinemann, 1981.

The Use of Cross-Cultural Myth in Soyinka's *The Bacchae of Euripides*

K. SANTHANAM

Redemption through sacrifice has been a major literary theme in all literature which evokes a universal appeal. There are myths and legends which go to prove the fundamental belief in expiation and redemption, both personal and collective. The concept of individual sacrifice leading to retribution and subsequent rejuvenation has been explored by Soyinka in a number of plays and poems. Soyinka introduces this theme of retributive sacrifice leading to expiation, in his adaptation of the *Bacchae* of Euripides also. Though Soyinka adheres to the main plot of the original, that of Dionysus' revenge of King Penthus who refuses to acknowledge his godhead and worship him, he has made certain additions of his own indicating a new dimension to the great classical tragedy. In this play, Soyinka has not only used the Greek myth but also has reinterpreted it in the African context, thereby establishing a link between classical tragedy and its modern counterpart. "Soyinka took the bones, and some of the flesh, of the original and completed it in such a way that his own ideas on power ritual, religion and tragedy became clear."[1]

In Soyinka's play, Tiresias, the blind prophet is seen chased and flogged by a mob. Obviously he has been chosen as the carrier for the New Year. Tiresias accepts the role willingly on his head to cleanse all the evils of the country. Dionysus appears on the stage and explains the meaning of the sacrificial ritual. Both the old king Kadmos and Dionysus have become votaries of the new God, Dionysus. Dressed in fawnskin, they are on their way to mountains to witness the rites of Maenads' worship of Dionysus. Penthus appears infuriated by the mad frenzied behaviour of royal women who indulge in orgiastic rites in the hills, since they also have become the followers of the new God. Dionysus casts a spell on Penthus, wins over him and leads him on to the mountains. Penthus, under the hypnotic power of God, submits to this plan. After placing Penthus on the top of the hill at his own request, Dionysus disappears. Penthus is seen by the frenzied hysterical women led by Agave Penthus' mother. They pelt stones at him till he falls down when he is torn to pieces by his mother. Agave, who ecstatically dances is proud of her victory laurel. "I have such news for you. You are the proud Father of brave daughters. . . . We have left our Shuttle in the loom, raised our sights to higher things. We hunt. We kill," (304) Kadmos arrives along with Penthus' dead body. Agave wants her son to come and see her crowning achievement. Kadmos cannot keep quiet. He asks his daughter to see the head which she has hoisted on the polls. Truth dawns on her. She screams and orders the head to be brought down. Suddenly she becomes very calm. She herself climbs the ladder and brings down her son's head. Agave in all her regal dignity accepts the responsibility and is prepared to face it.

Agave: Let no hand but mine be laid on him.
I am his mother. I brought him out to life
I shall prepare him for his grave. (306)

At this point, Tiresias appears on the stage. He says that Penthus has sacrificed himself for the sins of the country, voluntarily or otherwise. He has atoned for his own personal sin against the god and his sacrifice becomes not only inevitable but even necessary in the interests of the country. In the original Greek play both Kadmos and his daughter leave Thebes and wander about from country to country for the crimes committed against the royal throne. The final note of Euripides' play shows us the inscrutable ways of the God.

Soyinka has called his adaptation of the *Bacchae* as "A communion rite." Soyinka, by introducing certain changes in the original Greek play, has not only made the play "less Euripidean in essence, but also has brought about a rare synthesis of Greek and Yoruban myths and rituals."[2] The tremendous intellectual power of Soyinka is seen in the reinterpretation of the Greek myth to the modern times.

Soyinka, in his play, has made three major changes which help us in understanding the play as a "communion rite." These three changes involve (i) The nature of Penthus' regime (ii) The reinterpretation of the role of Dionysus (iii) The transformation of the end of the play from a tone of lamentation and sorrow to one of celebration.

The nature of Penthus' regime is suggested at the very opening of the play. Soyinka's Penthus appears to be very distinctive, being associated very strongly with death, repression and megalomania. The tyrannical regime of Penthus is indicated by a set which includes a row of crucified slaves and then by the abrupt and dictatorial manner which Penthus adopts. Whereas Pentheus of Euripides does not once use the word "order" in his opening speech, Soyinka's Penthus uses that word repeatedly, thereby showing his desire to control and dominate at all costs. This is evident from the brutal way in which he deals with the elderly Tiresias and an old slave. Penthus has established a tyrannical regime which involves a perversion of religious rites into a cruel sacrifice of slaves as scapegoats. In the opening scene, Tiresias takes on the role of the annual scapegoat for cleansing the country of its evils. As a seer, he knows that he has been implicated in the leadership of Penthus' reign. The tyranny is expressed by the suffering of the scapegoat on behalf of the entire nation. Actually this sort of suffering should be undertaken voluntarily by the ruler of the country. If the sacrifice and suffering are undertaken unwillingly it remains a meaningless suffering and death with no prospect of a new life or new beginning. The ruler's given life is not available for the renewal of the realm. It is for this reason Soyinka dramatises this moment of transition very elaborately in this section of the play. Penthus' sacrifice, though involuntary, shows his acceptance of the role as a spiritual leader. Only it is such an acceptance that makes meaningful the transformation of the end of the play. This transformation makes the play a happy communion rite symbolising rejuvenation and rebirth instead of the irretrievable loss we have in Euripides. The sacrificial death of Penthus brings in real ecstasy in Thebes. The blood that flows from his death transforms into a fountain of wine soaking the land in fruitfulness.

Soyinka has also incorporated ritualistic features which are evident from a close reading of the play. By introducing ritualistic and sacrificial elements into the structure of the play, Soyinka has established his links with the ritual roots of African theatre. This shows Soyinka's sensitive mind responding to ritual as a living reality in the African tradition.

The second major change relates to the role of Dionysus. Soyinka in his play presents Dionysus in more masculine and manly terms than what one finds in Euripides' version. Soyinka's Dionysus is a combination of Apollonian and Promethean qualities, in fact more Ogun-like whereas Euripides' Dionysus has a soft, even effeminate appearance. "Instead of the 'effeminate beauty' of Euripides' Dionysus, Soyinka talks of 'a being of rugged strength and of rugged beauty' and prepares the way for the manly temptation."[3] The God's opening speech shows no signs of revenge and stresses instead his wish to restore life. This restorative quality is very much evident, particularly towards the close of the play in Soyinka's Nigerian adaptation.

Soyinka's most daring alteration or innovation is seen at the end of his play. Suddenly from Penthus' severed head blood begins gushing out in powerful jets from all sides of the skull. Kadmos and the others present are shocked at the very sight, shaking in fear of Dionysus' renewed anger. But Tiresias goes forward allowing the stream to fall on his face. He smells it, tastes it and cries in excitement: "It is not blood, it is wine." Finally "the God of wine has won." Gods have forgiven the royal family. The play thus ends not on a note of tragedy, but on a note of joy and fruition. The final tableaux of a wine sprouting head clearly demonstrates the regenerative power of the sacrifice—even of unwilling sacrifice. The principle of regeneration through sacrifice has been present in all religions and so it is nothing new or unique in Soyinka's play. But Soyinka has made this aspect a distinctive part of his artistic sensibility. "He has found it in his culture and realised it very beautifully in the conclusion to his treatment of the Greek play in which a tyrant's blood fertilizes the country and brings in new life."[4] Soyinka's adaptation therefore goes beyond the note of catharsis, ending on a note of renewal or new life. His use of wine as a concrete image of rebirth is very significant in the play. For example, in the opening scene of the play we see slaves and herdsmen share a Jug of Wine that is passed round the group. Wine is identified with joy and fertility. And so when at the end of the play wine gushes out of the severed head of Penthus, Soyinka seems to suggest the rejuvenating power of wine. He seems to be saying that out of the horror has gushed the wine, thereby asserting the rebirth or renewal of life. The play's final affirmation comes out of his nightmarish experience that he went through in Nigeria and so his play is appropriately sub-titled "A Communion rite." Soyinka has an optimistic view that out of the most terrible rape of the nation joy can still emerge. Soyinka here refers to the dictatorial and tyrannical regimes led by civilized blackmen in Nigerian politics. He not only opposed these power seekers but also looked forward to a time when Nigeria can be free from such repressed regimes and people can feel the joy of freedom. So it is against this background of contemporary reality Soyinka's version of Euripides has to be seen.

Soyinka follows Euripides closely throughout the major part of the play. His own lived experience in Nigeria has helped him reinterpret and transform the myth. In fact "Soyinka sets the Greek myth inside the framework of his own response to the Nigerian reality."[5] in the hands of a mature artist like Soyinka, the adaptation of Euripides becomes highly creative and socially relevant particularly in the context of African situation.

NOTES

Textual passages cited here are taken from *The Bacchae of Euripides*, Wole Soyinka, *Collected Plays*, Vol. I (Oxford University Press, London, 1977.

1. James Gibbs, *Wole Soyinka* (London: Macmillan Modern Dramatists, 1986), p. 112.
2. Radhamani Gopalakrishnan, *At Ogun's Feet* (Tirupati: Sri Venkateswara University, 1986), p. 116.
3. K.E. Senanu "The Exigencies of Adaptation: The Case of Soyinka's Bacchae," *Critical Perspectives on Wole Soyinka*, ed. James Gibbs (London: Heinemann Educational Books Ltd., London, 1981), p. 109.
4. James Gibbs, p. 115.
5. Albert Hunt, "Amateurs in Horror," *Critical Perspectives on Wole Soyinka*, p. 114.

J.P. Clark's *Ozidi* and African Theatre

N. EAKAMBARAM

John Pepper Clark is a Nigerian poet, dramatist and critic, more a poet than a dramatist or critic. He belongs to the Ijaw people who live in the southern delta region where the river Niger flows into the Gulf of Guinea. For centuries they have lived as hunters and peasants for the land is fertile and gifted with copious rains. Farms and forests surround their homes and the people have an intimate knowledge of the life of nature.

J.P. Clark in his introduction to his collection of poems, *A Reed in the Tide* calls himself "that fashionable cultural phenomenon they call 'mulatto'—not in flesh but in mind!" in order to focus upon the encounter between the traditional Nigerian culture and the modern Western culture in his life and writing. This repeats the pattern of what was happening in Nigeria in the middle of the twentieth century. 1960 is an important year in the history of Nigeria for it is in that year Nigeria achieved its independence from British rule. Also its cultural renaissance began in that year, but this brought the conflict between cultures to a sharp focus more than ever.

Even as Nigeria awakened to the consciousness of its identity, J.P. Clark and so many young people of this period awakened to a new life. Clark was born in Kiagbodo in the Ijaw region of Nigeria in 1935, educated at Warri Government College, Ughelli from 1948 to 1954, and at the University of Ibadan from 1955 to 1960 for his Hons. in English Literature. He spent an year in 1962-63 as a post-graduate scholar at Princeton University, America. Since 1964 he has been a member of the department of English at the University of Lagos, and currently Professor of English and also a founding member of The Society of Nigerian Authors.

The Nigerian authors' choice of the English language for creative writing is understandable for it is a country where more than 200 languages are spoken, though certain languages like Hausa, Fulani, Yoruba, Ibo and a few others are used by fairly large groups of people. English is the official language of Nigeria, and it is the language of the educated, and it is being increasingly used by the people when they come together from different regions.

The use of English for creative writing by Nigerians has raised many doubts. Martin Esslin in his article "Two African Playwrights," in *Black Orpheus* in 1966 reviews the plays of Soyinka and J.P. Clark. He prefaces his discussion by granting that these two are "real masters of all its nuances . . . and very considerable artists in English," but goes on to observe:

> Here again the problem arises from the nature of drama itself. These plays are by Africans about Africans in an African social context. And they are, largely, about Africans who, in reality, speak their own African languages. (282)

Martin Esslin is intrigued why these playwrights write in English. He points out: "I am, in my own mind, not quite clear as to the reasons that prompt African playwrights to use English in preference to their own rich and highly poetic languages. Is it that they themselves are more at home in English?" (283) The assumptions that underlie Martin Esslin's question do not seem to be happy. And this question has been taken up by many African anglophone poets, dramatists and fiction writers.

Chinua Achebe in an article, "African Literature as Restoration of Celebration" (1990), points out the persistent crusade of the European to depersonalise Africa and denigrate the continent as an area of darkness. Then he goes on to the complex issue of the English language. He asks: "Does my writing in the language of my colonizer not amount to acquiescing in the ultimate dispossession?" (7) He recalls how at the age of thirteen he went to a public school modelled on British public schools and met for the first time a large number of other boys of his own age whose mother tongue was different from Achebe's Igbo language. These boys from the different regions of Nigeria had to use the English language in order to communicate with each other. Regarding the learning of English, he makes the following observation:

> It is simply not true that the English forced us to learn their language. . . . We chose English not because the English desired it but because having tacitly accepted the new nationalities into which colonialism had grouped us, we needed its language to transact our business, including the business of overthrowing colonialism itself in the fullness of time.
>
> Now, that does not mean that our indigenous language should now be neglected. It does mean that these languages must co-exist and interact with the newcomer at the present time and into the foreseeble future. For me it is not *either* English or Igbo, it is *both.* (8)

Achebe has effectively focussed upon the complex social context in Nigeria where many languages vie with each other and English comes in as a very necessary link language. The label that it is the coloniser's language need not confuse the issue. Many Nigerian authors like Soyinka, Achebe, J.P. Clark and others have preferred to write in English and reach large audience within and outside Nigeria. They have brought to bear on English the quality of an African sensibility, and the result has been a harvest of superb literary works.

Clark's verse plays like *Song of a Goat* (1961), *The Masquerade* (1964) and *The Raft* (1964) published in the volume *Three Plays* (1964) are unmistakably African, but the influence of Greek and Elizabethan drama and the poetic drama of T.S. Eliot may also be perceived in them. It is in *Ozidi* (1966) that he uses a wholly African experience, meant for performance in a village setting. In the prefatory note Clark tells us that

> The play is based on the Ijaw saga of Ozidi, told in seven days to dance, music and mime, and which I have recorded on tape and filmed with a grant from the University of Ibadan. I am now preparing the Ijaw and English text of the work for publication.

Clark's involvement with the Ozidi saga as told in the Ijaw community is for more than thirty years. He had not only listened to this story year after year, but developed a sustained interest in it. He wanted to preserve the saga material and also achieve a literary text out of it.

The Ozidi saga is the story of revenge that takes place in the village of Orua in the Ijawland in Nigeria. A council of the warriors and elders of Orua elect Temugedege, an idiot as their new king, their previous kings having died early. The renowned warrior Ozidi is Temugedege's younger brother. When Ozidi insists that the rights of King Temugedege must be honoured, the cunning warriors conspire against Ozidi and murder him and serve his head as a gift to the King. In this horrendous act of betrayal and murder the entire community of Orua is implicated and it needs to be cleansed. Ozidi's wife, Orea gives birth to a male child in her mother's house in another village. Orea's mother, Oreame, a notable witch, rears the boy into an agent of vengeance. When he grows up to be a warrior of great strength and cunning, he learns his name to be Ozidi. It is twenty years after his father's murder that the young Ozidi comes to Orua village, and with the help of the magic of his grandmother, fights against his father's enemies and kills them one after the other. These are epic battles described by the narrator in great detail and excitement. But after these challenges he is not able to live a peaceful life. He fights with and kills more people. He strikes down his own grandmother by accident and she is brought back to life. His fight with the Smallpox King proves to be formidable, but with the help of his grandmother he defeats his enemy and drives him out of Orua.

The story is noted not only for the heroism of Ozidi and the revenge motif, but for the variety of characters who enliven the story. There is even comedy alternating with the scenes of battle. Michael Etherton in his pioneering book *The Development of African Drama* (1982) points out how the Ozidi saga spread over the seven nights of its narration "evoke(s) for the audience, a whole community, a whole world together with its cosmos and special ambience 'where the land meets the sea and the sky'; and it is this community which is the focus of the story." (73) In fact, the Ozidi saga may be looked upon, to borrow a phrase of Achebe cited earlier, as "a literature of celebration" of the life of the Ijaw people in Orua and elsewhere. The word "celebration" is used here, as Achebe does, in a comprehensive sense to include the joys and sorrows of the community in its continued life in history.

The Ozidi saga exists in two versions: as a narrative told by a story-teller to the Ijaw groups, and as an enactment by a group of actors before Ijaw adience. Both the versions have received Clark's attention. He tape-recorded the story as told by a narrator in Ijaw language, then transcribed and translated it into English. He published this in 1977 as *The Ozidi Saga* with the Ijaw and English versions side by side along with an introduction. This is different from his play *Ozidi*. He also tried to catch the magic of enactment in a film made in 1964. He travelled with the film-maker Frank Speed in 1964 to Orua and helped him film the enactment of the saga. The film proved to be too long. Finally it was edited to forty-five minutes length and released under the title *Tides of the Delta* in 1964. There are also three long-playing records called *Songs from the Ozidi Saga* released by EMI on behalf of the Institute of African Studies, University of Ibadan. Clark's play *Ozidi* published in 1966, according to Michael Etherton, "reveals a two-fold commitment: first, to record the saga, and to preserve it, as accurately as possible, in its traditional narrative and performance forms; second, to transform it into a modern work of art." (69-70) Clark achieves a play-text out of the Ozidi oral epic material and it stands as a pinnacle to his involvement in the rich and colourful life of his people.

Even in the play *Ozidi*, Clark has retained the dual aspect of the saga by beginning with the narrative mode and moving on to the dramatic and concluding with the narrative again. The story-teller dressed in a white flowing skirt and tunic draws the attention of the audience and tells them of a problem in starting the play. He needs seven young virgin women to be bearers of food offerings to the spirits of the sea and "so establish between us a bridge." As the seven virgins come forth from the audience and take up pots of food, the orchestra of the master drummer, three side drummers and a horn blower, and the chorus of actors and dancers emerge singing, and a procession to the stream begins with the sound of drums and horn. At the stream the story-teller plays the role of the priest and offers the food to the spirits and prays to them: "Please give us good wives,/ Give us good children, and give us good money, too." Then the virgins go back among the audience, the actors and and dancers fall apart and take up positions on either side of their leader, and sing a praise song to the accompaniment of drums. As an old woman sweeps the floor in a ritual of cleansing, the story-teller asks her to leave, because "We can have important affairs of state to consider right now." The entire group become the Council of the State of Orua, and the narrator plays the role of Ozidi.

The story-teller is a mediator between the audience and the tragic life of Ozidi which is about to take place. His frequent references to contemporary persons and events are only strategies of relating the Ozidi saga to contemporary life, and thereby achieve the presence of the past in the life of the community.

It is also important to note the frequent use of music, dance, and ritual in the opening scene. Adrian A. Roscoe in *Mother is Gold: A Study in West African Literature* (1971) observes how "The dancing, ritual, and singing set a pattern which is continued throughout the play." (216) These conventions have been preserved in Africa over the centuries and their presence in the play makes it authentically African. The younger Ozidi is able to avenge his father's murderers with the aid of the magic of his grandmother, Oreame. It is only when Ozidi is possessed does he achieve his triumphs.

Clark has imposed a certain order on the materials from the saga for his play in five acts. While Act I takes place in Orua, Act II moves to Ododama, the village of Oreame, and the remaining Acts take place in Orua. But the play is far from the unified structure one finds in Greek drama. Adrian A. Roscoe notes:

> *Ozidi* is *not* in the classical tradition. . . . This is crowded drama, teeming alike with characters, scenes, and events. . . . If the characters in *Song of a Goat* are seen at one crucial moment in their lives, the central figures of *Ozidi* grow from youth to old age before our eyes: the hero indeed is not born until after the play has begun and, thereafter, we watch him develop from childhood to adolescence and manhood, and then fall to his doom. A static, marble-cold Greek quality is replaced by a frantic sweep of hot gory action , epic in its proportions and African in its abundance. (213-14)

In Act I the elders and warriors of Orua deliberately choose the idiot Temugedege as their King. When he insists that gifts must be given to him that are due, and Ozidi also declares that the King should not be bypassed, they conspire and call for a hunting expedition to bring gifts. In Scene 6 Ozidi's enemies, Ofe, Oguaran, Azezabife, and Agbogidi beat him to death for he is so protected by magic that bullets, spears, swords, and arrows cannot hurt him. Then they cover his head in coco-yam leaves and Ofe cuts off his head. In Scene 9 they present the head of Ozidi to his brother King Temugedege who stands dazed, and Orea breaks into a lament and cradles her husband's head in her lap.

In Act II, which consists of seven scenes, Oreame, Orea's mother, brings up her grandson to be a warrior of matchless strength, courage, and cunning. It is amusing to read some of these scenes in which Oreame, the witch, assumes terrible forms to frighten her grandson and then reveals herself. In Scene 5 the old man of the forest, Bouakarakarabiri, gives Ozidi "the mortar and pestle charm" to protect him. Soon the boy learns his name to be Ozidi, and the name reverberates in his consciousness as the name of his renowned father. A blacksmith forges a seven-pronged sword for him. Now the young Ozidi is fit to meet his father's murderers.

In Act III Orea returns to Orua after twenty years, with her son Ozidi and her mother Oreame to see her husband's house in ruins and her brother-in-law ("father-of-her-marriage") Temugedege in rags, and Ozidi "start(s) clearing the bush; on this spot/Let us raise again the compound of my fathers." In Scene 3 Ozidi learns the names of those who had killed his father and now his way is clear. In another scene Oreame prays to Goddess Tamara, "mother/ Of all mankind, moulder of earth, sky and sea," to bless Ozidi who is like a fledgling eagle— "go now and pluck out their eyes,/Pick the flesh clean off their bones." In Scene 6 in the public square of Orua, Ozidi and Azezabife fight a duel to death, as the people of Orua have gathered in support of Azezabife and his partners in crime. Even as Azezabife makes strategic retreats, Oreame casts a spell on him to stop, and asks Ozidi to cut him down and so he does. Clark omits Ozidi's fights with the other warriors like Agbogidi and Oguaran, and presents in Scene 8 the fight with Ofe. Ozidi relents under the ferocity of Ofe's onslaught, but Oreame revives him and almost paralyses Ofe. Then Ozidi defeats Ofe and cuts off his head in a frenzy. As people rush away, the old woman kneels down in confusion for her grandson is in a possessed state. With this retribution is complete.

The problem with Ozidi in Act IV is that he cannot settle down to the routine of life in peace time. His energies are so completely absorbed in warfare that he does not even feel hungry, or love some girl and get married. Orea is extremely unhappy over this but she is helpless. Ozidi provokes a fight with the seven-headed monster of a man, Tebesonoma and is trapped in a net, but Oreame who was away in her village comes to his rescue, and finally Ozidi slays his enemy. He also kills Tebesonoma's sister and newly-born child to prevent future retaliation. In Scene 4 he brings Odogu's wife home but is not able to love her and marry her. What follows in the next scene is a terrible fight with Odogu the Ugly who is also protected by "the mortar and pestle charm." It is like a fight between two equal armies. Finally, with Oreame's magical aid, Ozidi kills Odogu. In his frenzied state, he accidentally kills Oreame also. Clark makes a departure from his source in the Ozidi saga and leaves the grandmother to die.

Act V takes place after many years and presents Ozidi's encounter with Engarando, the Smallpox King with his retinue of Cold, Cough, Headache, Spots, and Fever, and his younger brothers Egirigiri and Okrikpakpa. Obviously, these are allegorical figures who have come to punish Ozidi. Though Ozidi survives their onslaught, he is left broken and desolate. Orea has become an old woman and she mistakes the spots on her son's body for yaws. The moment the people of Orua learn of the terrible visitation of the Smallpox King, they flee from the village and leave Ozidi to his fate. The Act consists of a twin scene with the play area divided into two parallel planes, one for the Smallpox King and his group, and another for Ozidi, Orea, and the village people. In fact, the group of the Smallpox King come singing and dancing as they arrive on the beach of Orua and the two acting areas mingle and separate as the action requires. As the dreaded visitors leave Orua in a brisk ceremonial dance, the story-teller returns as Ozidi with all the other actors in a long processional dance, "in which," according to the stage direction, "all spectators may join."

Ozidi is remarkable for the synthesis of the narrative-dramatic mode with the elements of ritual, dance song, mime, and music which are authentically African. As the story-teller suddenly turns into the elder Ozidi, and he dies, and a little later another Ozidi turns up to pursue the action of revenge, characters seem to be imbued with forces far beyond the span of a human life. The elder Ozidi who appears in Act I only is cast entirely in the heroic mould. His reputation as a warrior is splendid, and with his loving wife, Orea at home, the cup of life seems to be full. But conspiracy almost like an accident strikes him down. The lesson seems to be obvious that cunning politicians cannot bear the presence of a great man in their midst. The younger Ozidi is an instrument of revenge and at the same time of the cleansing of the community of Orua of the sin of being an accomplice in the killing of a loyal warrior.

When Ozidi overreaches himself, of course, with the active aid of Oreame, he is punished by the forces of nature. Orea's vulnerability at the death of the elder Ozidi is paralleled by Tebesonoma's sister's helplessness, and the younger Ozidi does not respect this sanctity of life. In fact, more than Ozidi, it is Oreame who goads him on to this atrocious action. Again, it is Oreame who breaks the charm that protects Odogu the Ugly, the wronged husband, and enables Ozidi to kill him. Oreame's witchcraft is both positive and negative. It promotes the restoration of a moral order, but in the later part of the play it turns away. And for all these unwanted killings, Oreame pays for with her own life. As Orea tell her son about his grandmother in the last scene:

> She grew wings, she walked on clouds, trespassed
> On sacred grounds, and for that you struck her down
> By the hand of one born of her own daughter.

But the question remains: what else could Oreame have done at the time of her grandson's battles? She is right up to the time of the completion of revenge, but in the later killings she supports the wrong-doer. Oreame's behaviour only shows that the ways of parental solicitude are strange. Further, the younger Ozidi, unlike his father, depends on women for his strength. He is not only reared by them, but for the success of his heroic deeds he needs the aid of his grandmother. Strangely enough, all his heroism does not enable him to partake of the pleasures of the home, of love and marriage, of a wife and children. Orea in Act IV, Scene 4 tells him:

> Leave the woman alone, Ozidi!
> Now there is nothing else you can do but kill?
> Oh, no more sleep for us again in this house.

When he is not able to possess Odogu's wife whom he has brought home forcibly. Ozidi's excessive heroism is punished with impotence and alienation. Orea's cry, "no more sleep," has a resonance far beyond the literal, and she lives to grow old and see her son punished by the Smallpox King. It is only her love which may save him in the end. Ozidi's heroism is like that of a meteor which burns itself out.

The language of Clark is poetic and has an impressive range of communication. It conveys the great sorrow of Orea at her husband's death or at her son's suffering towards the end, the great joy of Ozidi's triumphs over his enemies, the fiery spirit of the warriors in their cunning and in their bravery, the playfulness and intelligence of Oreame as she rears her grandson, and also the routine life of the people of Orua. The imagery is drawn from the life of the Ijaw people—farming, fishing, and hunting—and their land. Thus the language is rich and colourful and gives depth to the dramatic experience. The meaning of *Ozidi* keeps reverberating like the African drum long after we close the text which reenacts itself endlessly in our imagination.

WORKS CONSULTED

Chinua Achebe, 1978. "An Image of Africa. "*Research in African Literature*, 9.1: 1-15.

——. 1980. "African Literature as Restoration of Celebration." *Kunapipi*, 12.2: 1-10.

Ulli Beier, ed. 1967. 1979. *Introduction to African Literature: An Anthology of Critical Writing*. London: Longman.

J.P. Clark. 1964. *Song of a Goat*. In *Three Plays*. Three Crowns Book. Oxford: Oxford University Press.

——. 1966. *Ozidi*. Three Crowns Book. Oxford: Oxford University Press.

Commonwealth Literature. 1979. Introduction by William Walsh. Great Writers Student Library. London: Macmillan. 53-54

Contemporary Literary Criticism, Volume 38, 1986. Detroit, Michigan: Gale Reseach Co. 112-29.

Martin Esslin. 1966. "Two African Playwrights." *Black Orpheus*, 19 March: 33-39. Rpt. *An Introduction to African Literature*. Ed. Ulli Beier. 281-88.

Michael Etherton. 1982. *The Development of African Drama*. Hutchinson University Library for Africa. London: Hutchinson.

Christopher Heywood, ed. 1971. *Perspectives on African Literature*. Selections from the Conference on African Literature held at the University of Ife, 1968. London: Heinemann.

Adrian A. Roscoe 1971. *Mother is Gold: A Study in West African Literature*. Cambridge: Cambridge University Press. Selections in *Contemporary Literary Criticism*, Volume 38.

The African Voice—The Griot in Ayi Kwei Armah's *The Healers*

R.M.V. RAGHAVENDRA RAO

The imminent period of radical experimentation heralded by Camara Laye's *The Radiance of the King* (1954) in Kafkan techniques did not, however, affect the flourishing of the traditional African novel. Achebe supplemented the classical tradition of the novel, as Africa received it from Europe, with the linguistic resources from Ibo language. But by 1960s the influence of the modernist novel with its insistence on form and style began to be felt. Its focus shifted from the subject matter and the events being narrated "to the essential duplicity of form itself,"[1] as observed by Lewis Nkosi. Nkosi cites as instances of the new novel, Camara Laye's *The Radiance of the King*, Gabriel Okara's *The Voice* (1964), Wole Soyinka's *The Interpreters* (1965), Ayi Kwei Armah's *The Beautyful Ones are Not Yet Born* (1968), Kofi Awoonor's *This Earth, My Brother* (1971), Ngugi Wa Thiongo's *Petals of Blood* (1977), and Yambo Ouologuem's *Bound to Violence* (1968).

Set against Achebe's classical serenity in story-telling, and his art which conceals art, the narrative style of these novels cited may be modernist in the sense that there is a constant search for style. Nevertheless, their dominating obsession is with the simple act of story-telling, which draws its vitality from the perennial oral traditions of Africa. A striking example of the preoccupation of the African novel with the historical past as a theme and the time-honoured technique of oracular narration is

Ayi Kwei Armah's *The Healers*.[2]

Each of the five novels of Armah, namely, *The Beautyful Ones are Not yet Born* (1968), *Fragments* (1970), *Why are we so Blest?* (1972), *Two Thousand Seasons* (1973), and *The Healers* (1978) signifies a definite stage in his literary vision. The first three novels, however, found unpalatable by critics for their content and imagery, constitute a negative or destructive stage in Armah's career. *Two Thousand Seasons* and *The Healers* form a constructive stage, for the reason that they both demonstrate the triumph of truth over falsehood. If the experimental novel of Africa is towards greater complexity and an opaque texture, as observed by Robert Frazer, in novel after novel, "Armah's prose style has become increasingly transparent, the amount of ambiguity, for example, having notably declined."[3]

The gradual change in the narrative technique of Armah is towards the oral tradition of story-telling which is a pointer to the artist's growing awareness of the social context and his affirmation of the communal consciousness and racial memory, as in *The Healers*.

The Healers focuses on a historical moment at a certain stage in the development of the Asante empire. Subtitled "an historical novel," it falls within the implicit framework of Armah's novels—within his consciousness of historical events and a period or a vast span of time, as in *Two Thousand Seasons*. Yet, *The Healers* goes beyond chronology or a European calendar, by portraying the cultural paradoxes in the life of the Asante community and its encounter with the colonial experience. It dramatizes the pride and humiliation of these people bewildered by the impact of a technically superior colonial force, during the years 1873-74, or, the period of the second Asante War. More importantly, it juxtaposes the mainstream of Asante life, i.e., its preoccupation with martial arts with the "healers."

The canvas of characters of *The Healers* consists of Asamoa Nkwanta, a general and a ruler of battles opposed to his own nation at war, Densu, a staunch believer in the healers, his mentor and the healer Damfo, the princess Araba Jesiwa, and the advocates of falsehood such as Ababio and Buntui who are the "manipulators." Its action consists of the clash between the healers and the manipulators within the Asante, the division among several tribal kingdoms and the wars that follow.

Recorded fact and fiction constitute the plot of *The Healers*. It weaves its way through several narrative shifts from history to philosophical debate spread over its seven parts, of six subdivisions each. Far from making the plot episodic, such divisions only contribute to the novel's richness of narrative levels and techniques, consisting of oral narration, and epic proportion, besides time-patterns and repetition. As Ahmed Saber observes, "All these narrative methods are used to enhance the communal theme of the novel."[4] And more significantly, quite in keeping with the growing concern in his fiction to reach a larger readership, Armah uses the narrative technique of the Griot in *The Healers*.

The term, "griot," according to Ruth Finnegan, "was presumably originally a translation of the Fulami *gaoulo* (wandering poet or praiser) or Wolof *gewel* (poet and musician), it is now popularly used as a term to refer to almost any kind of poet or musician throughout at least the French-speaking areas of West Africa."[5] The griots were narrators of genealogies, reflectors of public opinion, and professional free-lance poets, or the *azmaris*, in Ethiopia. Within the tradition of West African drama, "in the Savanna regions there is a long tradition of professional historians-cum-entertainers (the *griots*),"[6] to cite E.J. Collins. Armah himself was very much influenced by the importance of the griots, before writing *The Healers*. In a book review of Niane's *Sundiata*, Armah stated that "the *griot* was a thoroughly professional artist trained to use the subject matter of his people's history as the raw materials of his art. The artist, the griot, was therefore the historian and story-teller, both."[7]

In *The Healers*, Anona is the griot who claims to be a "descendent of masters in the arts of eloquence." (2) He keeps invoking his masters for inspiration; he invokes the Sotho author Mokopu Mofolo (1876-1948): "Send me words, Mokopu

Mofolo." (52)

In narrating the history of the Asante people, the Esuano streams, the wide land between them and the "rituals of remembrance," (4) Anona shifts from the third person, to the first person plural pronoun, "our people," (4) thereby placing himself within the historical account. The conscious use of "we" and "our" in the midst of an effortless style of disarming closeness with the reader, establishes the novelist's commitment to present a collective voice. The queen mother Efua Kobri who accepts a state of surrender to the British, says, "we have done so many things to bring the curse of God on our own heads, and God is punishing us." (279) She interprets a historical event in terms of causes and effects based on the African faith and beliefs. Thereby, the characters of *The Healers* are not a mere ensemble of chronological events, but reflectors, interpreters, and participants in a collective life.

The narrator's sense of history expresses itself not only in terms of a collective past but also a personal past. The latter is brought out by the characters themselves or in the narrator's accounts about them. Araba Jesiwa's account of herself to Densu is an instance:

> Do you understand, Densu? I had been told it was the right thing to do, that I should marry one of the royals because I was one myself. Had I listened to my real self, I might have wondered why. But I was not in the habit of listening to myself. I feared I would go wrong. I did what the others said was right. (69)

The personal past and the historical past are blended so well that the very function of the griot seems to be one of maintaining a sense of continuous flux. While remembering his boyhood, Densu tells of the appearance of the first white man at Esuano, "This too he remembered: in his twelfth year something strange had happened. A white man had arrived at Esuano." (157) The griot thus is a repository of historical event, a conveyor of historical consciousness and a mouthpiece of obsession of the individual with a personal past steeped in fear and anxiety, as is the case with Densu. According to Ahmed Saber, these constant interactions in the individual's consciousness "serve to convey Armah's perception of history as a continuous flux of competing social forces."[8]

The narrative technique of the griot includes several traditional stylistic forms of expression such as oral histories, folk tales, local beliefs and customs of the Asante people—all endowed with an aesthetic as well as a didactic purpose achieved through the griot's technique of repetition.

Repetition serves as a stylistic device and a rhetoric of the epic in *The Healers*. There is an expression of invective and irony in the portrayal of certain characters. For instance, in describing Glover, the narration runs as follows:

> Glover the godlike, Glover the white man descended among the black people to do magical wonders. . . . Here he was, Glover the father of the Hausa fighters, protector of loving slaves. Here he was, Glover, he whose word was alone sufficient to inspire thirty thousand black men to rush delirious into the open jaws of death. (255)

Thus, by adopting the technique of repetition for reprobation, Armah adds yet one more dimension to the range of oral patterning and to the effectiveness of the rhetoric of the epic.

Besides, in *The Healers*, the griot uses grandiose language, epithets, statements of morals, invocations and proverbs. Some of the characters are of heroic proportion: the scope of the novel is vast; there is invocation to the Muse (to Mofolo), and one reads catalogues of kings, chiefs, tribes and rivers and kingdoms.

The Healers, however, is an epic of the entire African consciousness as reflected in the griot's stylistic patterns. The griot is the detached narrator as well as the sharer of the collective life, portrayed in the novel. He speaks for the roots of the African creative expression and the continuum of African life in cyclic patterns, in rhythm of speech, and music.

In *The Healers* the griot also vindicates truth and justice and the role of healers and their believers, or followers. We hear his voice of authority in the passage on the role of the healers; it is a call for collective involvement.

> Healing is work, not gambling; it is the work of inspiration, not manipulation. If we the healers are to do the work of helping bring our poeple together again, we need to know that such work is a work of a community. (270)

The community's collective voice is further affirmed when, at the end of the novel, Ama Nkorma, the healer-woman asks Damfo, "Does it not amuse you, that in their wish to drive us apart the whites are actually bringing us work for the future? Look!"

The Healers thus takes us backwards to the African oral tradition only to reaffirm its efficacy and relevance to the need of the African people to stand, speak and "look" collectively. *The Healers* speaks to the African reader, "with an authentic African voice—the griot's voice."[9]

NOTES

1. Lewis Nkosi, *Tasks and Masks: Themes and Styles in African Literature* (London: Longman, 1981), 54.
2. Ayi Kwei Armah, *The Healers* (London: Ibadan, Heinemann, 1978). Further references to this text are given in parentheses.
3. Robert Frazer, *The Novels of Ayi Kwei Armah* (London: Heinemann, 1980), x.
4. Ahmed Saber, "Narrative Techniques and the Oral Tradition in Aye Kwei Armah's *The Healers*," *The Griot: Focus on Black Literature*, vol. IV, Nos. 1 and 2 (Winter/Summer, 1985), 73.
5. Ruth Finnegan, *Oral Literature in Africa* (Nairobi: O.U.P., 1976), 96.

6. E.J. Collins, "Comic Opera in Ghana," *Ghanaian Literatures*, ed. Richard K. Priebe (New York: Greenwood, 1988), 61.
7. "*Sundiata*, An Epic of Old Mali," *Black World*, Vol XXIII, No. 7 (May 1974), 51-52; 93-96. Ahmed Saber's "Narrative Techniques," which perceptively deals with some of the oral techniques in *The Healers* refers to this factor as a powerful influence on Armah. (The author of this paper owes several of his insights into the African narrative traditions to Saber's article).
8. Saber, 77.
9. *Ibid.*, 80.

Okonkwo and His *Chi*

Notes towards a mythological approach to Achebe's novels

S.K. SARMA

Chinua Achebe's *Things Fall Apart*[1] is rich in significance and can be approached from many viewpoints. One can study it from the anthropological viewpoint, the viewpoint of clash of religions, Christian and pagan, and notice the defeat of an African worldview that served the communities for centuries; one can view it from the geo-historical stand point, as a chapter in increasing British hegemony, as an attempt at Britain's acculturation of the African tribes, and see in it the arrogant advance of European culture over all that had been pristine and innocent. One can approach it in terms of clash of ideologies, a clash between two value systems, one traditional, socio-religious, and the other modern, racial-evangelical, and watch the systematic demolition of the African psyche and African ethos. It can also be studied as a tragedy, a clash between free will and predestination, with emphasis on the role of *hubris* in the development of Okonkwo the protagonist. He emerges as the representative of the Igbo culture, possessing the very best of the qualities glorified by that culture, valour, fearlessness and physical powers. The calamity and the tragic events at the end raise the protagonist to the levels of classical Oedipus or Orestes, or King Lear. But we also notice that Okonkwo is primarily motivated by fear—the fear of being considered weak and feminine. Yet it is neither his pride in his own mightiness nor his fear of being called weak, but a freak accident, of killing a kinsman at the funeral of a village elder which results in his exile for seven years. On the other hand, it is his native traits of impulsiveness and awareness of his might which prompt him to cut down the court messenger. When we analyse the last events closely, we find that he was not prompted to suicide by contrition over the act of killing, nor by fear of retribution at the hands of the white man, but by the awareness that when he acted precipitously, the community had broken into tumult instead of action. It shows how far Okonkwo is isolated from the community, an isolation which had occurred during the period of his exile, though it could not have been caused by it. Surely, we cannot at this point in the novel say that his action was prompted by pride or arrogance: he must have felt the pressure of the tribal values needing an urgent succour. And it is the knowledge of his isolation that drove him to suicide. In this, perhaps he comes closer to Hardy's Henchard than the classical tragic heroes.

It is also possible to approach the novel from the mythological viewpoint and study Okonkwo's actions and reactions from the perspective of Igbo tribal beliefs. *Chi* the spirit being has a central place in Igbo mythology.[2] It stands as a counterpart to the human being; for one of the fundamental aspects of the Igbo belief is that wherever Something stands, Something Else stands behind it. *Chi,* as the individual manifestation of the Supreme Creator (Chukwu), is responsible for the traits, gifts and talents of the individual. Man strikes a deal with his *chi* in everything. If one grows too proud or too big for his shoes, he would be overthrown by his *chi*. And if all divinities conspire to destroy a man, they can do so only if his *chi* consents to it. In spite of this unprecedented veto power, *chi* cannot be said to possess absolute powers. This is the second fundamental aspect of Igbo belief: no one is permitted absolute powers. The initiative passes on to man: "if a man agrees, his *chi* agrees," goes the saying. But even man cannot be bestowed absolute powers. The check is provided by another potent force, the will of the community. "No man, however great, can win judgement against all the people." Sometimes a man may fall into apparently unmerited adversity. But according to the belief, this could only be the result of the primordial agreement between the man and his *chi*, for they believed in a fundamental justice in the Universe, so that somehow a man happens to be responsible for his own misfortunes. (This comes rather close to the Indian belief in the theory of Karma, while the relationship between the duo of *chi* and the Supreme *Chi* reminds us of the relationship between the universal soul and the individual soul in Indian philosophy.) On the other hand, one may suffer from a bad *chi* who says no when the man says yes. Or the inexplicable misfortune may be because the man is trying too late to alter the prenatal bargain he had struck with his *chi*. (Does this remind us of the conflict between free will and predestination?)

Okonkwo must have been enjoying the support of his *chi* while he prospered in the community and built a place for himself and progressed from title to title and attained an honoured place among the people of Umuofia. Never challenging his *chi*, nor possessing overweaning pride—only once does he mock at another saying that the meeting was for *men*—but he is quick to apologise, (24) he enjoyed good rapport with his *chi*. He was picked out to collect the fine of the girl and the boy Ikemeruna from Mbaino because of his place in the community. But, beating his wife during 'the Week of Peace' and killing Ikemefuna when he had been warned against participation in the ritual killing because it would appear to be weakness in him, were crimes against Ani, the Earth Goddess, for which she could destroy the community itself. These violations seem to disturb the easy relationship between Okonkwo and his *chi*. Only thereafter does the calamity of accidentally killing a kinsman at Ezeudu's funeral occur, leading to his exile. According to the Igbo belief, this accident could not have occurred without his *chi* permitting it: "No matter how many divinities sit together to plot a man's ruin it will come to nothing unless his *chi* is there among them." As a result, his prosperity and his place in the community are gravely affected.

But Okonkwo's willingness to expiate his sin does not

seem to satisfy the goddess. Her anger is visited upon the community, apparently. The inroads Christianity makes into the tribal faith coincides with Okonkwo's exile; and the inability of the community to stem the rot, a certain amount of falling apart, indicates the weakening of the community as a force. Is it possible that all this is because of Okonkwo's crime against Ani? Achebe presents a similar situation in *An Arrow of God* where the fields of the natives wither while those of the Christian converts prosper, because of Ezeulu's refusal to declare the planting season at the right time. If Ezeulu sulks over his imprisonment and refuses to eat the yam, arrogating to himself the powers of decision, it cannot be said that Okonkwo acted in pride and arrogance in killing the kinsman. One cannot somehow lay the blame on Okonkwo. His action at the end, hasty though it was, was quite in accordance with the traditional values. It was an act of conviction, almost religious, and the end vindicated the character of Okonkwo, who emerges as the lone representative of the Igbo value system while the entire community lay around him in a shambles.

The village elders had refrained from any confrontation with the new religion because the ancients had not laid down any form of action, for they had not visualized such an eventuality. When Okoli, a new convert, reportedly killed the royal python, they said it was a matter between the killer and his god; they did not presume to interfere. (145) Okoli's subsequent death was seen as a vindication of their faith in the gods' ability to take care of themselves. But when one of the ancestral spirits is unmasked in the public, and thus 'killed' by Enoch, they could not allow things to rest; they go and burn the church. For this the village elders are put in prison and a penal fine extracted from the community; they return home and call for a meeting to decide the course of action, at which meeting Okonkwo kills the trespassing court messenger; and when the gathering breaks up in tumult, Okonkwo goes and hangs himself.

Can we say that the community was as hasty in burning down the church as Okonkwo was in killing the messenger?

Perhaps there is a difference. A concerted action of the community, however thoughtless, is still communal and has the sanction of tradition; while an individual's action does not enjoy a similar support. Facing the unknown enemy is an unfamiliar crisis for the Igbo community, while Okonkwo is not facing any personal crisis. However strong he may he, he cannot win against the will of the poeple. Though it is not pride or arrogance but a sense of despair which prompts him to action, he should have deferred to the will of the community. Unfortunately, at this point in the novel, there does not seem to be any community with a will of its own, for him to act for or against, or to defer to. Nothing throws stronger light on this falling apart of the community than the picture of the stalwart Okonkwo standing as the sole upholder of the value system, even at the risk of defying the laws of the community. He pays for the defiance with his death, yet he holds the attention of the reader with his desperate stance. The reader finds no difficulty in identifying with this protagonist.

Such an analysis of the novel, and especially the character of Okonkwo, seems to strengthen our appreciation of the novel as a tragedy, while at the same time it throws feelers for further investigation into a comparison between the role of the Christian Free Will on the one side and the Indian concept of Karma and Rebirth on the other with the Igbo view of the protagonist. The idea of Free Will, perhaps semi-consciously worked into the fabric of the novel by Achebe, explains the developing image of the self-made Okonkwo as a harsh tyrant, and even suggests the presence of *hubris*. But an analysis of the novel from the Indian perspective could only be fanciful, since Achebe could not be aware of the close parallel between the Igbo and Indian philosophical systems. It may still be worthwhile pursuing it.

NOTES

1. Chinua Achebe, *Things Fall Apart*, Arnold-Heinemann, 1958.
2. Chinua Achebe, '*Chi* in Igbo Cosmology' in *Morning Yet on Creation Day*, Heinemann, 1945, pp. 93-103.

Myth and Symbolism in the Novels of Chinua Achebe

S.A. KHAYYOOM

Every community has a rich mythological heritage and every creative writer uses the native myths to narrate contemporary events, to expose public follies, and to explain the problems and mysteries of life and death. Achebe, working from his mixed heritage of Igbo birth and Christian upbringing and interpreting Igbo myths and their relevance to contemporary living, attempts to rehabilitate the African psyche damaged in its cultural encounter with the West.

Africa, for many an outsider, is a gloomy phenomenon, a dark continent of dense forests, cannibals and wild life, a fantasy world inhabited by bushmen, witch-doctors, mysterious beings and a literally swinging Tarzan. But it is only a myth. This literary stereotype, i.e., years of denegration, is countered by many African writers with a sense of pride and commitment. Africa is no longer an imaginary continent, a "trackless wilderness" devoid of meaning. It is rich in culture and mythology and its inhabitants are endowed with "unique and novel" potentialities. African culture is a donor culture, not a client culture.

The 'Negro' is branded as socio-cultural inferiority. For Julia Peterkins the "Negro" is "ignorant, indigent, shiftless, immoral" and for some "the unspoiled child of nature, the noble-savage, carefree, spontaneous and sexually uninhibited." But elders of the so-called primitive society are wisemen, repositories of ancestral wisdom, imbibed from remotest antiquity to pass on to their progeny. They are heroic explorers, children not of darkness but of the Sun and are conscious of their beauty, endurance and charm. "Black is beautiful" is their defiant and self-inspiring slogan to counter the Western impression of Negro as "slave, savage and outcast."

Negritude is a cultural and political myth used by Achebe in his novels. This ideological movement, an existential philosophy, according to Leopold Sedar Senghor, is not only a way of being but also a way of living. it attempts to redefine the ethnological aspects, and re-evaluate Africa within a non-western framework. It has helped in rediscovering Africa and African and in establishing a new social order. It tries to liberate the man of colour from himself and has rejected what the white world stands for, but it has degenerated into an intolerant and arrogant racialism. Achebe, like Negritude writers, in his anthropological novels tries to glorify and celebrate what is good in the African past but unlike them appears to have denounced the unhealthy traditions and inhuman rituals and practices by exposing the social evils, and political injustices, in his other two novels dealing with modern Nigerian society.

A man of two worlds is another African myth that Achebe has dealt with in his novels. Obi and Odili are of two worlds, products of hybrid culture. Nanga and Ezeulu have a strong affiliation to the native tradition but are drawn to the alien culture. Okonkwo too is aware of the inevitable change in Umuofia. Achebe in *No Longer at Ease* describing the life in Lagos presents a moving picture of traditional rural life suffering the onslaughts of modernity. He has portrayed the African myth of the man of two worlds suffering from intolerable internal stresses, liable to desert his career and virtues at a crisis. The ending of the novel is far more than a mere case study of Obi, an isolated individual.

Achebe in his novels has outlined the Igbo-creation myths. Umuaro believes in Ani, Mmo—the spirit-world, High God or Creator, and Earth-Mother. But, the High God and Earth Mother fail to change their fate and protect the villagers from starvation and death. "Chi," "Personal spirit," "god within," of everyman and woman is sometimes equated with the Christian concept of 'free will.'

Time is the matrix and functional structure of the human self. It constitutes and liberates the human self. St. Augustine conceived of Time as an existential 'present' informed by the past and future in memory and expectation. The traditional concept of Time in African fiction is entirely different from that of the Western. African time (tribal concept) is a two-dimensional phenomenon with a long past, a present and virtually no future. Instead of numerical calendars, the traditionalists have phenomenon calendars in which significant events or phenomena constitute time. To them, time is meaningful at the point of the event. We are told that the death of Okuata, the first-wife of Ezeulu, occurred when the evil moon was sighted with legs upward in the sky, a bad omen. Africans have a lunar calendar, "hunting months," "weeding months," "hot months," "the beans harvest months" etc. When the community is agricultural, it is the seasonal activities that make "the agricultural year." The traditional cyclic time is punctuated by festivals—Pumpkin Leaves Festival, New Yam Festival in *Things Fall Apart.* According to Spengler time in an African sense has little to do with actual blocks of time as measured in a Western sense but rather with human values and human achievements."[1] In *Arrow of God* the story begins on "the third nightfall since he began to look for signs of the new moon." The arrival of the Moon is watched and welcomed with religious fervour. The pattern of events in the novels of Achebe suggests the linear view of history in his imaginative rendering of colonial history. The details of events establish the Igbo chronology. The market weeks, moons, harvests, festivals, seasons and lunar years can be contrasted with the Western weeks, days, dates and twelve-month years.

In *Things Fall Apart*, we are told that Okonkwo was "eighteen" when he threw the cat, a great wrestler, which was "twenty years or more ago," which means he was about forty at the beginning of the novel. But we are told that Ekwefi, Okonkwo's favourite wife, is fortyfive and that it was thirty years ago that she loved him when Okonkwo threw the cat. From this we may assume that Okonkwo was nearly fifty. This "discrepancy" does not matter at all to the tale, as in Igbo chronological system, there is no need to establish definite dating of events. The confusion in Okonkwo's age is due to Achebe's use of English phraseology suggesting Western time. In *Arrow of God* Captain Winterbottom uses the phrase "more than two years ago" to describe the event which might have taken place in 1919. The past which is two years ago is expressed as "the more recent past" or "mgbe gara aga" (in the time past). The more distant time is expressed as "mgbe dianya mgbe" (in the more distant time past). Such expressions show more of the spirit of the Igbo system of telling time than the Western one.

For Africans, religion is individual as well as communal and they have a more personal concept of God. The gods in Achebe's novels are more immanent than transcendent. The godly powers in the novels help and guide the people in restoring the social order. Achebe emphasizes this vital aspect of the myth—Divinity grounded on human realities—in his novels. Achebe conceives of God primarily as a moral postulate. He is de-mystified in *Arrow of God* and is brought right into the midst of villagers' fights with the creation of Ulu as the protector of Umuaro to instil the collective will to work for prosperity, progress and freedom. Umuaro gods—Ulu, Eru, Idemili etc.—are, like Greek gods, not above jealousy and spite.

Achebe consciously employs symbols and symbolistic techniques in his novels. He has used with economy, traditional rituals and conventions to symbolise the Igbo society. The offering and breaking of kola nut is a sign of good will. The guest, who visits the obi of the villager, is given a lump of white clay to draw his personal emblem at the threshold as a mark of respect and friendship. By killing himself Okonkwo has desecrated the Earth goddess. The power of Ndichie, i.e. of Egwugwu, elders of the village, is vested in their symbolic wearing of ancestral masks. The villagers, instigated by

Okonkwo, ransack the church in Umuofia when a Christian convert desecrates one of the Egwugwu by tearing its mask. In the death of Okonkwo, Achebe symbolises the death of what is traditional in Africa and the collapse of the entire society. Obierika of alien disruptive forces says:

> The white man is very clever. He came quietly and peaceably with his religion. Now he has won our brothers, and our clan can no longer act like one. He has put knife on the things that held us together and we have fallen apart.[2]

In *Arrow of God*, Ulu symbolises the spirit of political cohesiveness combating the external forces to safeguard the freedom and integrity of the clan. The chief deity also symbolises the enlightened consciousness of the people of Umuaro, and Ezeulu is his supreme spokesman. The theme of *Arrow of God* has elaborated the destruction of the tribal world but through a more sustained character. Achebe in alternate chapters depicts the two worlds which could never come closer. Native folktales and legends woven into the novel do not have much relevance to the plot but create the atmosphere to strengthen the traditional life. The threat of collapse of the old order because of its exposure to a superior order is stated by Achebe in a proverb:

> . . . a man who brings ant-ridden faggots into his hut should expect the visit of lizards.[3]

Ezeulu, Nwaka, and Captain Winterbottom are symbolic agents of this tragic development. The role of the whiteman in the collapse of the traditional society is conceived as much symbolically as historically.

Most of the characters in the novels of Achebe are symbolic of the age, society and country. Obi, as a young Nigerian graduate, suffers and faces his sticky end under the pressure of economic and cultural change. Odili Samalu in *A Man of the People* perhaps symbolises the Nigerian spirit who has survived the sacrifice at the "new shrine," one who has anticipated the emergence of the new generation to look for a better future shaped by the wisdom of the past as well as the present. Nanga and Odili symbolise the social contradictions in the novel.

Achebe in *A Man of the People* portrays on a grand scale the infectious nature of corruption in Nigeria—politics in the army, in civilian life and in the whole of rural and urban environments. He seems to be cynical about his new Nigerian society. Odili is more than a single character, as observed by Donald Weinstock:

> If Odili's story indicates anything, it would seem to be that the amalgamation of British and Nigerian modes of life has effected no more than the description of the best in both cultures . . . and what is doubly disturbing, the Africans, by partaking of the European experience (for nearly a century now), have put on all of the contemporary spiritual problems of Western man as well.[4]

Achebe in his novels intentionally draws white characters as flat characters, for they do not totally represent any people, but together they symbolically stand for forces of an alien culture, to which the central characters respond. In *Things Fall Apart* Rev. Brown and Rev. Smith are different beings though they exhibit militancy as colonial administrators guarding the interests of Imperial Rule. In *No Longer at Ease*, Mr. Green, Obi's boss, is a dull representative of the old colonial system. Captain Winterbottom, the District Commissioner in *Arrow of God* is a foil to the ambitious Chief Priest who tries to demonstrate his temporal authority on Umuaro. And in *A Man of the People* we have the American couple interested in "things" African, representing a generation. Achebe has deliberately made his white characters just phantoms playing insignificant roles in the history of their province, and he gives them names suggesting anonymity.

The locale of *Things Fall Apart*, Umuofia, is symbolically named after the bush people who inhabit it. Umuofia means "children of the forest." But 'ofia' has different connotations in modern Nigeria: Ofia is 'bush,' uneducated, uncontaminated by European urbanism.

The symbol is also used sometimes as a suggestive device. Though Umuofians come to know that white men who are not albinos exist, they have not heard of the Aro expedition. The Abame massacre, in the words of Obierika, "Abame is no more" is a fictionalised history. Abame has been wiped out by the whiteman as a reprisal for killing one whiteman named Dr. J.F. Steward. This act of vengeance is given the form of the Abame incident in the novel.

Achebe's novels are perceived differently by the readers and critics, and are thus symbolic. The title *Things Fall Apart* is suggestive of the crumbling of the ancient order. Symbolically there is a "cultural chasm," "external conquest, internal collapse" and the novel also suggests a kind of power struggle. *Arrow of God* also deals with a similar theme, but here Achebe has symbolically demonstrated the triumph of the new faith over the superstitious old order, maybe the liberation of soul from the grip of the old order. In the novels, the role of the whiteman in the disintegration of the tribal world is conceived as much symbolically as historically. Achebe demonstrates that the whiteman's presence merely acts as a catalyst in the ruin of the old order, which is mainly due to the antagonistic forces within the clan.

Achebe's fictional art goes beyond argument and propaganda and traces the decline and fall of the Igbo utopia towards the political nightmare of corrupt society. Achebe renders meaningfully in his novels the Igbo encounter with historical change and crisis and uses creatively his sense of the pastness of the present and the presentness of the past. Achebe as an innovator of modern African fiction with universally acclaimed literary merits in him is a writer to be reckoned with.

NOTES

1. Charles Larson, *The Emergence of African Fiction* (Bloomington and London, 1971), p. 106.
2. Chinua Achebe, *Things Fall Apart* (African Writers Series, London, Ibadan: Heinemann Educational Books, 1956), p. 160.
3. Chinua Achebe, *Arrow of God* (London: Heinemann, 1964), p. 178.
4. Donald J. Weinstock, "Two Swarms of Locusts: Judgement by Indirection," *Studies in Black Literature*, II, 1, 1971.

Pre- and Post-Colonial Society in Achebe's Novels

N. RAMA DEVI

The African novel, in general, is known for its depiction of various cultural tensions and conflicts arising out of a clash between tradition and modernity, the real and the occult, and so on. But it is the conflict between the individual and the society and the way in which it is resolved that seems to lend a typical African flavour to the African novel, thus distinguishing it from its European counterpart. To be explicit, in the event of a clash between the individual and the society, the scores are more commonly settled in favour of the individual as against the society in the European novel, as could be seen in the case of Dorothea in George Eliot's *Middlemarch*. And the reverse is always the case in an African novel in which society, the larger entity, emerges triumphant as against the individual who dissociates or delinks himself from the society to assert his pride and individuality. Here the question is not so much about the right or wrong of the individual's convictions or credentials as about the necessity of the people to adhere to the society with its roots in a traditional faith. The people happen to be aware of the unifying and sustaining capacity of the society. They believe and depend on its power to hold them together as the 'centre.' It is because of this 'centre,' they could survive the hardest of times. With this kind of confidence being laid on the society, it is not surprising to see even the closest of the individual's associates and kinsmen deserting the individual in the event of his clash with the society. The individual has practically no stakes against the society.

A study of Chinua Achebe's two novels, *Things Fall Apart* and *A Man of the People,* with special emphasis on the aspect 'individual vs. society' brings to the fore, not only the predicament of the individual in revolt against the society but also shows how the individual and society cease to exist as two real entities with the passage from the pre-colonial situation to the post-colonial situation.

Things Fall Apart, set in a pre-colonial situation, depicts Okonkwo's rise and fall. As Okonkwo claims himself a champion of the Igbo tradition, in his fall, we visualise a proud and stable society gradually disintegrating and being destroyed by the encroachment of an alien society. Okonkwo was the Igbo hero, in that he showed exceptional bravery, firmness, even greatness of soul. "He was well-known throughout the nine villages and even beyond. As a young man of eighteen he had brought honour to his village by throwing Amalinze, the Cat."[1] Amalinze was the great wrestler who remained unbeaten for seven years. Okonkwo was proud and was the brave man of Umuofia in every sense. His life was dominated by the local customs and the fear of being called weak. It was this fear which prevented him from being openly affectionate towards Ikemefuna, his foster son. He even goes to the extent of cutting him down with his matchet (for, "he was afraid of being thought weak,"[2]) which was the most telling of his aberrations. Okonkwo, though he was a staunch follower of the local customs, happened to flout certain norms of his society in significant aspects and in doing so brings many of his own ills upon his head. But this flouting "is not, in terms of the design of the book, merely incidental or accidental, these deviations are highly significant and are made into major issues so that in the process the norms are all the more clearly defined."[3] He is twice punished for his crimes against Ani, the earth goddess, first, when he beat his wife during the 'Peace Week' and next, when his gun killed Ezelu's son by accident. For this, he accepted the penalty and went into exile to his motherland, Mbanta. By the time he returned to rebuild his reputation in Umuofia, he finds the whiteman's rule established. He tries to stand as a rock against invasion.

His helplessness and frustration are clearly evident in his blind fury in which he almost kills his son Nwoye, when he comes to know that the boy had been frequenting the missionaries. And when the boy forsakes his parents and becomes a convert, a "sudden fury rose within him and he felt a strong desire to take up his matchet, go to the church and wipe out the entire vile and miscreant gang."[4] He wants his people to go to war.

Okonkwo, who turned out to be the odd man out in his community even before there was any confrontation with the whiteman, now becomes even more alienated from his community in his attempt to assert his individuality. And his only recourse is to rebellion, against the whiteman. But the traditional society being aware of its weaknesses does not want to confront the whiteman's power. And, Okonkwo, during one of his solitary confrontations with the white power, kills the messenger of the district commissioner. And in the question of his clansmen, "why did he do it?"[5], he realizes that the world to which he belonged is dead and no longer with him, and he hangs himself knowing fully well that it was an abomination, an offence against the earth. His clansmen, while approving his more moderate ambitions, do not hesitate to criticise him for his excesses and deviations in urging him to follow the accepted social restraints and expectations.

In Okonkwo's fate is illustrated and dramatised the dire consequences that the individual has to face for having turned his back on the society in the African situation. As has earlier been pointed out, the question that comes up is not one about the integrity of Okonkwo as an individual.

Okonkwo, no doubt is a worthy person, a man of conviction with a strength of character. But in his attempts to assert his own convictions, he goes too far, to the extent of dissociating himself from the society, the macrocosm. For this, a streak of pride, a sense of "hubris" within him is responsible. It impairs his sense of acknowledging the supremacy of the society—the "centre" which holds them all together. For this, he has to pay too heavy a price, "dying like a dog." Obeirika, one of his closest friends, says, "that man was one of the greatest men in Umuofia. You drove him to kill himself; and now he will be buried like a dog. . . ."[6] Obeirika's words suggest that Okonkwo had to die like a dog because of his pride which delinked him from the society. If only he was one with the society and acted from within, many of his clansmen would have been with him even if it meant going against the whiteman, and he would have been given a ceremonial burial by his people, one of the privileges which everyone yearns for.

Achebe thus presents the conflict between the individual and the society and its consequences in a pre-colonial society in a neutral fashion without taking sides either with the individual or with the society. As a disinterested and neutral observer he succeeds in exposing the good and evil prevailing in the native African culture and an alien culture. As David Cook points out, "He prefers to reveal the darker side of both traditions as well as the better side and leave us to draw our own conclusions."[7] He neither romanticizes the Igbo society nor villifies the Christian European behaviour as a whole. Achebe thus writes about a clan which at the beginning, "thought like one, spoke like one, shared a common awareness and acted like one"[8] and traces the process of the falling apart of the society and the loss of a unified pattern as outside forces play on the new generation.

A Man of the People, on the other hand, depicts the post-colonial situation in a modern African state which is on its way to sever its ties with the traditional past. In this novel, Achebe exposes the inadequacies in a society which is losing its traditional moorings and also the opportunistic tendencies of the local, newly emerging politicians. Achebe takes a strongly satirical stand to show how the local traditions and customs are exploited by these politicians to meet their selfish needs. Achebe, here, is dealing with a country that has entered the age of the isolated individual confronting a mechanical administration.

The action of the novel is unfolded from the point of view of Odili Samalu who hates and has opted out of politics. Chief Nanga, ironically called "man of the people" as Browne is popularly referred to in V.S. Naipaul's *The Mimic Men*, does nothing but exploit the people. When he visited the village Grammar School, he promises Odili—who hails from Nanga's village—a trip to England on a scholarship for further studies. Odili, in his pursuit of the promised scholarship, goes to the capital and stays in Chief Nanga's house as a privileged guest. Though Odili happens to hear terrible things about Chief Nanga and the contemporary politics, he fails to take Nanga seriously because of the latter's openness and kindness towards him. But when Chief Nanga seduces Odili's girl friend, Elsie, Odili is deeply hurt and decides to retaliate and prevent the marriage between Chief Nanga and Edna—to marry whom he had already paid the bride-price and whose higher studies he had been financing. The seduction becomes intolerable because it is viewed as an instance of social indiscretion on the part of Nanga and not merely as something that affects a person personally. As a first step in his retaliatory path, Odili goes and joins hands with Maxwell Kulamo, a lawyer and his classmate at the Grammar School, who is now the leader of the Common People's Convention, a political party formed by certain people disillusioned by the tactics of Chief Nanga and others. In the elections Chief Nanga's party is to encounter a major threat from the CPC. But things are so managed by Chief Nanga and his private army that Odili is hospitalised just before he files his nomination papers and Maxwell is killed by Chief Koko's thugs on the day of the election. Chief Nanga's party comes back to power. Writing about the cynical attempt by political opportunists to make use of the tradition of unity to meet their own ends, Achebe says,

> A man who has just come in from the rain and dried his body and put on dry clothes is more reluctant to go out

> again than another who has been indoors all the time. The trouble with our new nations . . . was that none of us had been indoors long enough to be able to say "To hell with it." We had all been in the rain together until yesterday. Then a handful of us—the smart and the lucky and hardly ever the best—had scrambled for the one shelter our former rulers left, and had taken it over . . . and . . . they sought to persuade the rest . . . that the first phase of the struggle had been won and that the next phase—the extension of our house—was even more important and called for new and original tactics: it required that all arguments should cease and the whole people speak with one voice and that any more dissent and argument outside the door of the shelter would subvert and bring down the whole house.[9]

But soon after Nanga and his party's accession to power, the private armies formed during the election period, having disbanded after the elections, turned berserk and staged minor battles with which began a major reign of terror, and it culminated in the Army officers' taking over of power and the dismissal of the Government. The novel ends with the abolition of all political parties by the Army and the situation in the country returning to square one—suggesting the impossibility of establishing order in the state—which is more due to the indifferent attitude of the people than due to the corruption of their leaders. Achebe's satirical powers are at their best when he sums up the selfish attitude of the public as:

> "Let them eat": was the people's opinion, "After all when white men used to do all the eating did we commit suicide?" "Of course not, and where is the all-powerful whiteman today? He came, he ate and he went. But we are still around, the important thing then is to stay alive. . . . if you survive, who knows? It may be your turn to eat tomorrow. Your son may bring home your share."[10]

From that we notice, "survival of the fittest" seems to be the popular motto, with each one waiting for his chance to plunder. The irony actually is turned not only against people like Nanga, the great opportunist, but also against the "high-minded" people like Odili, the small opportunist who goes into politics to pay off a private grudge and who, in fact, has very little idea of the forces he is playing with.

Thus by the time we come to the post-colonial situation, there seems to be radical transformation in the entire scenario, a tilt in the balance. With the new politicians taking over political power, we find corruption and self-interest creeping in. The colonial politician who is elected to establish order in the state creates nothing but disorder as only "destruction comes with his emergence and is a condition of his power."[11] As against the pre-colonial situation where the society emerges as the victor and the sustaining force of the clan, in the post-colonial context, the society as an entity ceases to exist. And with the "centre" having no existence, there is no scope for any scheme of values to operate. People have allowed the politics to be westernized only to the extent of learning to serve the self first. In fact, the concept of "people" or society as an organic community has receded, with the individual becoming an abstract entity and with no enduring ideology or scheme of values operating as a cohesive force to unite the individuals and render sustenance to them. The novel as such seems to suggest that there are limits beyond which the communal will cannot operate meaningfully.

NOTES

1. Chinua Achebe, *Things Fall Apart* (London: Heinemann Educational Books, 1966), p. 3.
2. *Ibid.*, p. 55.
3. David Cook, "The Centre Holds—A Study of Chinua Achebe's *Things Fall Apart*," *African Literature*: *A Critical View* (Longman, 1977), p. 67.

4. *Things Fall Apart*, p. 139.
5. *Ibid.*, p. 184.
6. *Ibid.*, p. 187.
7. "The Centre Holds," p. 68.
8. Aigboje Higo, ed., "Introduction," Chinua Achebe's *Things Fall Apart*, 1965, p. v.
9. Chinua Achebe, *A Man of the People* (London: Heinemann Educational Books, 1978), p. 37.
10. *Ibid.*, p. 144.
11. V.S. Naipaul, *The Mimic Men* (London: Penguin, 1983), p. 36.

Ngugi and the New Historiography

C.R. VISWESWARA RAO

Though Ngugi's essays in *Homecoming* published in 1972 reveal the growing influence on him of Frantz Fanon,[1] and *Petals of Blood* and the play co-authored with Micere Mugo, *The Trial of Dedan Kimathi,* show the Fanonian emphasis on the peasantry and the land as the source of cultural strength and political change, as early as in *Weep Not, Child* (1964), *The River Between* (1965), and *A Grain of Wheat* might be seen Ngugi's cultural nationalist orientation influenced by Jomo Kenyatta's *Facing Mount Kenya* (1937), his determination to establish the worth of Kikuyu culture and customs, and further, his fictional concern, of the kind of Achebe's, for an even-handed portrayal of the colonial encounter. Lewis Nkosi's observation[2] which relates largely to South African writers—that an overwhelming emphasis on realism as the form and protest as the subject of fiction has weakened the artistic persuasiveness of African fiction and his plea for experimenting with the techniques of traditional African story-telling in the manner of Amos Tutuola's *Palmwine Drinkard* (1952) have indeed a great relevance when Ngugi's work—espeically an early novel like *Weep Not, Child*—is examined. In spite of a commitment to a Marxist analysis of society evident in his later work, Ngugi's view of literature redeems itself from being reductionist to the extent of considering literature as propaganda. But rather it implicitly adopts, at least in the early works, Terry Eagleton's assertion that "art is so ideologically powerful precisely because it isn't just propaganda."[3]

Ngugi's first three novels, *The River Between* (1965; drafted in 1960), *Weep Not, Child* (1964; drafted in 1962), and *A Grain of Wheat* (1967; completed in 1966), form something of a trilogy in the chronological progression in which they trace events from the female circumcision controversy which reached its climax in 1929 and led to the growth of Gikuyu independent schools (*The River Between*), through the Emergency (1952-56) imposed in order to suppress the movement commonly known as Mau Mau (*Weep Not, Child*), to the critical moment of Independence (*A Grain of Wheat*).

A novel which challenges the Kenyan youth to identify the salient features of their heritage, *Weep Not, Child* looks ahead in the direction of the later play, *The Trial of Dedan Kimathi* (1976), which examines the past in the light of the present in an attempt "to assess the enduring legacy of Mau Mau to independent Kenya,"[4] and not in the direction of *Petals of Blood* which contains allusions to Mau Mau, to distant African past and the black diaspora in a mode of examination where the present is looked upon in the light of the past. Though his critics accuse Ngugi of lack of artistry in his more recent, "committed" writing, that is, after *A Grain of Wheat* from where he "ceased to be a creative writer" and wrote mere "propaganda,"[5] a fact worth noting about Ngugi is that he unravelled oral history and analysed physical and linguistic evidence in order to present a coherent historical account. In *Petals of Blood*, Ngugi's narrator observes thus: "Just now we can only depend on legends passed from generation to generation by the poets and players . . . supplemented by the most recent archaeological and linguistic researches and also by what we can glean from between the lines of the records of colonial adventures."[6] Ngugi thus attempts an extensive cultural interpretation through his novels by posturing, as his later works more tellingly relate, an interrelationship between literature and history on the one hand and history and myth[7] on the other thus contributing to the richness and vitality of postcolonial Africanist historiograply. The task to which Ngugi committed himself was national interpretation which, as a literary-historical artist who has been extensively quoted by social scientists to defend their contentions, he undertook in the spirit of carrying out what the American scholar St. Clair Drake described as the "sacred duty . . . to redeem our race through the written word."[8] And the written word, in its discovery and literary recovery in terms of a seizing upon the "usable past" of the Africanness of African literature relies on orality, the reservoir and repertoire of tradition, modes, models and norms of African literature. The African writer's literary strategy aims at suggesting this alterior tradition characterized by the way in which orality is embodied in writing in order to make explicit the historical and cultural imperatives of which fiction is a byproduct. It is an exercise in defence of African culture against the imperialist thrust of contemporary literary theory and critical methodologies (as portrayed in *Towards the Decolonization of African Literature*.[9] It is a kind of reaction against imperialist discourse which, while trying to "decenter" a text, uses European ideologies of language and textuality to reinscribe the very canonicity of those texts. As an example for western theoretical analysis of oral cultures might be cited Michel de Certeau's argument that "ethnology"—a description of non-literature societies through narrative means—articulates contemporary social organization. He associates the oral with the primitive. In a polemical essay entitled "The Language of African Literature," Ngugi invokes a communal childhood with diurnal rounds of magic, folktales around the fire after sunset and the happy labour in the fields which betokened heritage, in spite of the alienation of the land:

> We spoke Gikuyu in and outside home. I can vividly recall those evenings of story-telling around the fireside. It was mostly grown-ups telling the children but everybody interested and involved. . .
>
> . . . Co-operation as the ultimate good in a community was a constant theme.
>
> . . . The language of our evening teach-ins, and the

> language of our immediate and wider community, and the language of our work in the fields were one.
>
> And then I went to school . . . and this harmony was broken. The language of my education was no longer the language of my culture.

This is an organic representation of Ngugi's own orally-based Gikuyu tradition, and he inscribes this oral as indicative of a former golden age, though this portrait of a holistic community, its shared cultural accoutrements are close indeed to an imperial vision of the child-like African innocence emanating from African writers such as Isaak Dinesen and Elspeth Huxley. But what is important in Ngugi is the way the oral is contextualized and it structures his "oral literature"—to use an "oxymoronic neologism" employed by Ngugi himself. His oral model incorporates the communal, verbal networks of the present through which his characters and communities exchange political and immediately contemporary information about those in complicity with economic neo-imperialism.[11]

It is in this respect that the theme of heritage and education explored in *Weep Not, Child* stresses, not so much the uncertainties and ironies inherent in the situation between 1952 and 1962, but the need for the collective approach as different from self-assertion on the part of the individual. Ngotho, at the centre of the protest from first to last, outlines the protest against the colonial situation by a passionate recourse to the orality associated with the idea of land as a time-honoured heritage. *The River Between* states this idea. Chege in that novel tells the youthful Waiyaki that the Gikuyu believe that Murungu bequeathed the land to them at the beginning of the world, and Ngothe hands down this myth to his children in *Weep Not, Child.* Ngotho suffers a loss of this heritage which bound the family together linking the living and the dead in an unbroken continuity:

> And yet he felt the loss of the land even more keenly than Boro, for to him it was a spiritual loss. When a man was

> severed from the land of his ancestors where would he sacrifice to the creator? How could he come into contact with the founder of the tribe, Gikuyu and Mumbi?[12]

Ngotho owed it "to the dead, the living and the unborn of his line, to keep guard over this *shamba.*" (31) He felt he was an insepa-rable part of the farm but for Mr. Howlands the land gave a sense of victory whenever he walked through it, for he alone was responsible for "taming this unoccupied wildness." (31) Both Ngotho and Mr. Howlands suffered a deprivation, a deprivation caused by war, that is, by the European civilization overpower-ing them in this impenetrable darkness. The land brings them uneasily together but shows how infallibly apart they are. Through a series of family sittings an account is given of this theme of heritage, the dreams and aspirations of Ngotho and his conflict with Boro, a pattern of the Mau Mau hero, and the expression of a society's growing self-awareness that is built up through an atmospheric quality which the oral tradition suffuses the narrative in. Boro, "bruised in mind" and in the spirit, in the process ("All the wrong done to the people was concentrated in the plaintive voice of Boro" [75]) anatomizes the harshest dimensions of the Mau Mau struggle, which Ngugi says is a central and catalytic event in the struggle for Kenyan independ-ence and not merely a manifestation of local Gikuyu national-ism. The Europeans spoke of it as a barbaric and atavistic rever-sion.[13] Boro, whose mission ultimately degrades to one of exact-ing vengeance, says thus to his lieutenant:

> 'Why then do we fight?'
>
> 'To kill, unless you kill, you'll be killed. . . . It's a law of nature. The white man too fights with gas bombs, and everything.' . . .
>
> 'What great cause is ours?'
>
> 'Why, Freedom and the return of our lost heritage.'
>
> 'Maybe there's something in that. But for me Freedom is meaningless unless it can bring back a brother I lost.

> Because it can't do that, the only thing left for me is to fight, to kill and rejoice at any who falls under sword.' (*Weep Not, Child*, 102-3)

Between Ngotho's musings based on a faith in legend and tradition and Njoroge's experiment in emancipation through education in which the entire community shares a faith, Boro's idealism shaped by a war-torn psyche provides a narrative pattern in which the present is the warp and the past is the woof, to borrow expressions from David Cook.[14] An interplay between different periods is achieved, to some extent as in *A Grain of Wheat* where the worn-out technique of the flashback is replaced by this technique of interplay assured by a community outlook and shared enthusiasms transmitted through the traditional African device of orality.

Though Ngugi is starkly realistic about the problems he identifies, as for example, the Asians' dominance over the small African traders, the novel encourages us to adopt a tolerant perspective on man's delinquency even through its penetrating vision of human sadness. This makes the final point not in tragic terms but in a positive demonstration of an alternative to destruction. Herein comes the educational theme and the associated vision of a unity of response in a human situation which might cut across racial distinctions but is subordinate to economic pressures. Kaman, apprenticed to Nganga, tells Njoroge bitterly: "Blackness is not all that makes a man. There are some people, be they Black or White, who don't want others to rise above them. They want to be the source of all knowledge and share it piecemeal to others less endowed. . . A rich man does not want others to get rich because he wants to be the only man with wealth" (21) In an atmosphere of internecine conflict evident in the conversation of the school boys and an anarchic, marauder-ing tendency giving a sinister touch to the uprising, Howlands with his assertive desire to reduce things to obedience, expresses his gratification thus:

> The blacks were destroying the blacks. They would destroy themselves to the end. What did it matter with him if the blacks in the forest destroyed a whole village? What indeed did it matter except for the fact that labour would diminish. (97)

It is against this background that Njoroge's education, his dream of accomplishing the redemption of his society are placed. In imagining a rosy future through the power of education, he is like Waiyaki in *The River Between.* Education for him is the fulfilment of a wider and more significant vision embracing the demand made on him by his kith and kin and the entire village. The shambles of the guerilla war will be sublimated, as he assumes, by means of his role as a saviour of the tribe. The conflicting elements of Gikuyu society have one common ideal, the ideal of knowledge:

> Whatever their differences, interest in knowledge and book-learning was the one meeting point between people such as Boro, Jacobo and Ngotho. Somehow the Gikuyu people always saw their deliverance as embodied in education. (104-5)

Njoroge's hope for himself and his people ("He saw himself rebuilding the whole country, [104-5]) his sense of mission, coupled with his recognition of the violence and uncertainty surrounding him in an atmosphere of war, insecurity, betrayal, and family disintegration show forth only a bleak hope and when confronted by Mwihaki, he clings to a vague hope and a naive vision of the promised land ahead for the Gikuyu: "Surely this darkness and terror will not go on for ever. Surely there will be a sunny day, a warm sweet day after all this tribulation, when we can breathe the warmth and purity of God." (106) What is significant in Ngugi's art at this stage of his evolution is the interlacing of the traditional Gikuyu myth and the Biblical tradition. Very subtly traditional and acquired religions are interrelated.

Njogore's belief in the future for his family and his village rested not only on a hope for and through sound education but also on a specific identification:

> a belief in a God of love and mercy, who long ago walked on this earth with Gikuyu and Mumbi , or Adam and Eve. It did not make much difference that he had come to identify Gikuyu with Adam and Mumbi with Eve. To this God, all men and women were united by one strong bond of brotherhood. (49)

That moment of disillusionment when Njoroge steps off the tarmac to reach the place where he has decided to commit suicide, his pursuit of education seems futile. And that road without a beginning and an end from where he moves, that dominant reminder in Kipanga of colonialism and "progress," serves as an apt image of an unformulated future and directionless movement of the society at large. But this image of the shiny tarmac road is less evocatively employed than the image of the ridges and the Honca River in *A Grain of Wheat* where it is a part of the structural symbolism of the novel. From the path of self-annihilation and from a sense of remorse for having run away from his responsibility towards a father who in an act of resolving a spirit of negation said, "Fight well. Turn your eyes to Murungu and Ruriri. Peace to you all—Ha! What? Njoroge look . . . look-to-your-moth—," Njoroge moves towards a final renunciation of self-destruction and cowardice. His finding of courage—expressed in the novel through a "fundamentally African art of understatement"—betokens a merger of the public and the private themes, as David Cook and Michael Okenimpke consider it,[15] in the sense that a possible rehabilitation of Njoroge in the social whirl is suggested.

The result of the African art of understatement in the fictional realm is that in *Weep Not, Child* the role played by the Mau Mau insurrection in gaining political sovereignty for Kenya is only dimly apprehended, for the stress on the educational theme in a way subordinates the political perspectives. The popular Marxist-inspired social ideals are therefore projected in the later work through a form of art—the drama—which is communal and through which the sordid dreary world is illuminated to larger groups of people collectively. The immediacy of impact which Ngugi sought to achieve was possible in *The Trial of Dedan Kimathi* (1976), a work that purports to contribute to the revision of Kenyan history which Ngugi regards as essential to his country's liberation from colonial legacy. In this commitment to the tracing of "the history of the inarticulate,"[16] Ngugi calls attention to his rediscovery of "the creative nature and power of collective work"[17] and bids farewell, in an attempt to forge the still uncreated conscience of the race, to writing in English foı he can "directly, have dialogue with peasants and workers" by "not only writing about peasants and workers but . . . for peasants and workers."[18] In newer literatures the pressures of nationality can be compulsive, and the creative artist, while transforming the raw materials of art into an act of communication, somewhat obscures the significance of the statement that "the value of literature is not to be judged by the yield which it offers the social historian."[19]

NOTES

1. Frantz Fanon, *The Wretched of the Earth* (Harmondsworth: Penguin, 1967), and *Black Skins, White Masks* (1959; New York: Grove Press, 1967).
2. Lewis Nkosi, *Home and Exile* (London: Longman, 1983), p. 132.
3. Terry Eagleton, *Marxism and Literary Criticism* (London: Methuen, 1976), pp. 163-4.
4. Carol M. Sicberman, "Ngugi Wa Thiong'o and the Writing of Kenyan History," *Research in African Litterature*, Vol. 20, No. 3 (Fall 1989), p. 350.
5. Peter Darling, "'Exiled' Dissidents Come under Fire," *Weekly Review*, 26 October 1984, p. 7.

6. Ngugi, *Petals of Blood* (1977; New York: Dutton, 1978), pp. 67-68.
7. An objection to Ngugi's promoting myth as history is discussed for example in Thomas Fleming, "Inventing Our Probable Past," *New York Times Book Review*, 6 July 1986, I, p. 20.
8. William R. Ochieng, "The Scholar and the Populariser," *Weekly Review*, 22 December 1978, 3 (Review of St. Clare Drake's *The Redemption of Africa and Black Religion*). Cited in Carol M. Sicberman, p. 361.
9. Chinweizu, Onurecheka and Ihechuku Madubukie, *Towards the Decolonization of African Literature* (Washington: Howard University Press, 1983).
10. Ngugi, "The Language of African Literature," *Decolonizing the Mind: The Politics of Language in African Literature* (London: Heinemann, 1986), pp. 10-11.
11. I owe this argument to Craig Tapping, "Voices off: Modes of Orality in African Literature and Literay Criticism," *Ariel: A Review of International English Literature*, Vol. 21, No. 3, July 1990.
12. Ngugi Wa Thiong'o, *Weep Not, Child* (London: Heinemann, 1964, rpt. 1987), p. 74. Subsequent references are to this edition.
13. An account of it is to be found in Donald L. Barnett and Karari Njama, *Mau Mau from Within: Autobiography and Analysis of Kenya's Peasant Revolt* (New York: Monthly Review Press, 1966).
14. *African Literature: A Critical View* (London: Longman, 1977), p. 96.
15. *Ngugi Wa Thiong'o: An Exploration of His Writings* (London: Heinemann, 1983), p. 67.
16. Arnold Temu and Bonaventure Swai, *Historians and Africanist History: A Critique* (London: Zed., 1981), pp. 3-5.
17. Ngugi, *Detained: A Writer's Prison Diary* (London: Heinemann, 1981), p. 76.
18. Emman Omari, 'Ngugi Wa Thiong'o Speaks!: "I am Not above the Contradictions Which Bedevil Our Society,"' *Weekend Standard*, 28 August 1981: I, 15. Cited in Carol Sicberman, 'Ngugi Wa Thiong'o and the Writing of Kenyan History,' *Research in African Literature*, Vol. 20, No. 3, Fall 1989, pp. 364-65.
19. B. Rajan, 'Identity and Nationality,' *Commonwealth Literature:*

Unity and Diversity in a Common Culture, ed. John Press (London: Heinemann Educational Books, 1965); rpt. in *Considerations*, ed. Meenakshi Mukherjee (New Delhi: Allied, 1977), p. 2.

Politicizing Language: The Relevance of Ngugi's Rejection of English

S.V. SRINIVAS

In this paper I shall attempt to examine the limitations of anti-imperialist writings in English, in the context of post-colonial countries. I shall argue that the "choice" of English or any other European language is a political one. In this regard I am in complete agreement with the Kenyan writer Ngugi Wa Thiong'o who says: "The language question cannot be solved outside the larger arena of economics and politics, or outside the answer to the question of what society we want."[1]

My contention is that the language problem in post-colonial societies is inherited from colonial societies. The history of the language problem dates back to the introduction of English language and literature into the curriculum as a part of the longer colonial educational enterprise.

The teaching of English was introduced as a state sponsored programme in colonial India in 1835.[2] The success of this experiment encouraged the British to introduce similar programmes in their other colonies, including those in Africa.

Historically the role of English education was to consolidate colonial domination and to strengthen (or even to create) the native elite. Creation of the collaborationist bourgeoisie was an impotant part of the colonial strategy of control, and colonial education was one of the methods by which this strategy was realised.

With independence the national bourgeoisie replaced the

colonial bourgeoisie and, as has been observed by a number of intellectuals including Fanon and Ngugi, the new rulers failed to introduce structural changes in the systems of administration and exploitation. The national bourgeoisie, preoccupied as it was with the scramble for privileged positions which were vacated by the colonizers, failed to address themselves to the problems in the economic and social spheres.

The colonial education system, which earlier provided the manpower for administration, was retained without any major changes. In the post-colonial context this system helps in the reproduction of the ruling class. This class, as Ngugi argues, in his fictional and non-fictional works, acts as the caretaker of imperialist interests in erstwhile colonies, resulting in a situation that has been categorised as neo-colonialism. Neo-colonial societies are formally independent but are dominated, politically and economically, by imperialist powers.

The interrogation of the privileged position of European languages in post-colonial African societies has been resisted and countered by African writers and critics who use these languages for their literary production and analyses. In his essay, "Return to the Roots," Ngugi recollects the 1960s debate in the pages of the journal *Transition* which amply demonstrates the tendency among intellectuals to view the use of the English language as inevitable.[3]

In his essay, "Thoughts on the African Novel," Achebe, addressed the problem in the following manner:

> there has been an impassioned controversy about an African Literature in non-African languages. But what is a non-African language? English and French certainly. But what about Arabic? . . . Is it then a question of how long the language has been present on the African soil? If so how many years should constitute effective occupation? For me it is a pragmatic matter. A language spoken by Africans on African soil, a language in which Africans write, justifies itself.[4]

Achebe thus attempted to free himself of the controversy, to avoid questioning *how* English and French came to stay on "African soil" and *which* "Africans" write in these languages. When the concept of "non-African languages" is put to such a severe test by Achebe, it is indeed surprising that the notion of the "African" is accepted so uncritically by him. Achebe's "pragmatic" justification of English and French is a result of his anxiety to defend these languages. Significantly, the "imapassioned controversy" has been summarized in one single paragraph and hereby dismissed and/or resolved.

In spite of Achebe's dismissal of the problem, it is not as if he does not attempt to find his own solutions to the language question. Achebe's use of Ibo proverbs, which has recieved much critical attention, is an attempt at reconciling the use of English, with its cultural baggage, with a social context that is very different from that of the First World. More interesting is the Nigerian writer Amos Tutuola's attempt. With only a sixth-grade education, he has written a number of prose narratives, the earliest of which *The Palm Wine Drinkard* is considered to be the first African novel by some critics. It begins as follows: "I was a palm-wine drinkard since I was a boy of ten years of age. I had no other work more than to drink palm wine in my life."[5] Tutuola's complete disregard for 'correct' English can be interpreted as a kind of resistance to the language which has in the process of its propagation launched an onslaught on indigenous languages and cultures.

Post-colonial writers have, through their literary production in European languages, launched attacks on not merely imperialism but also the indigenous ruling classes, which are the immediate causes for the post-independence betrayal of hope. Both Ngugi and Achebe have repeatedly argued that the writer has a social responsibility in that he ought to participate in the struggles against imperialism and other systems of exploitation. Ngugi remarks in *Decolonising the Mind*: "We as African writers have always complained about the neo-colonial economic and political relationship to Euro-America." However European languages severely limit the size of the audience, as Obi Wali has pointed out, since they are available only to those sections of the population which have had a chance to learn these languages in educational institutions.

The inability to communicate with the lower classes is a problem only for those writers like Ngugi who believe that a revolutionary social transformation can be made possible by the active participation of the working class.

It is ironic, however, that the radical critique of imperialism and post-colonial ruling classes in African literature has as its audience precisely those classes which are least interested in questioning the existing power relations. Ngugi's remarks on "African literature" of this kind are noteworthy. He asks,

> to whom was it (the petty bourgeoisie) directing its list of mistakes made. . . ? The imperialist bourgeoisie? The petty bougeoisie in power. . . ? It sought another audience, principally the peasantry and the working class or what is generally conceived of as the people.[6]

The post-colonial bourgeoisie, which is an overprivileged class is unlikely to play a constructive role in radical reform movements which would result in the loss of their political and economic power.

By writing in a European language, the writer in question also perpetuates the strategy of exclusion that resulted in the creation of the intermediary class in the first place. The production of such literatures, no matter how radically anti-imperialist, is situated within an elitist framework. This literature is, as Obi Wali pointed out, a dead end and an end in itself for there is no way in which it can contribute to the struggles aimed at dismantling existing systems of exploitation.

The point that I am trying to make is that anti-establishment literature in the languages of the ruling classes is a product of colonial and post-colonial elitism. It betrays the class origins and limitations of its producers who express a desire for change but do not bother to address the classes which are capable of bringing it about.

In this context Ngugi's decision to begin writing in Gikuyu is of enormous significance. Ngugi was arrested on 31 December 1977 by the Kenyatta regime for participating in the production of the highly successful play, *Ngaahika Ndeena (I Will Marry When I Want*, in English). The play itself was banned on 16 November 1977. Ngugi spent about a year under detention without trial. He decided to write a Gikuyu novel while in prison and did in fact write it. His first Gikuyu novel *Caitaani Mutharabaini*, translated as *Devil on the Cross*, was written on toilet paper.

Having taken an anti-imperialist stand and recognising that the peasants and workers, "have built Kenya," he realised that as a writer he was incapable of reaching them if he continued to use the English language. This is a significant move as he has successfully explored an alternative to the production of what he himself contemptuously calls "Afro-European literature." He has also problematized the "choice" of language and demonstrated that it is indeed a political one.

While literacy poses a challenge to *all* written forms, Ngugi's first Gikuyu novel found an audience even among the illiterate. It was read aloud for the benefit of those who could not read and some even paid to *listen* to the novel. These possibilities are not open to literature in European languages.

His decision is an expression of solidarity with the peasantry and the working class; a tribute to the struggles waged by them against imperialism and its local agents, and a recognition that the intellectual justifies his/her radicalism in alliance with these classes which make revolutions.

Not all writers can be expected to begin writing in the vernacular. Only those who share Ngugi's political views would see the existence of African literature in European languages as a problem. There could be writers who have lost their familiarity with the vernacular due to the education which suppresses non-European languages. This only points to the magnitude of the problem and the urgency of resolving it.

The literary scholar, Edward Said, points out that in the west,

> colonialism is seen exclusively as an experience that has ended, and about which any claims about or reparations for its damages and consequences into the present are dismissed as both irrelevant and preposterously arrogant.[7]

Writers like Ngugi and Achebe have challenged this view. They have shown in their writings that the ravages of colonialism have to a large extent determined the quality of life in post-colonial societies. The existence of an Afro-European literature in the post-colonial context is itself an example of the incompleteness of decolonization. When we view decolonization as a continuing phenomenon and not something which was completed with the transfer of power, the challenging of the privileged position of European languages can be seen as a part of this ongoing process.

By politicizing the question of language, Ngugi shows how it can become a crucial area of struggle. Since no one would contest that perpetuation of domination is a political question, and since Ngugi's analysis has shown us that language is an important means of perpetuating domination, neither language nor the culture it belongs to can be seperated from the political realm. Ngugi's intervention, as a writer, has to do with the interrogation of linguistic dependency. In deciding to write in Gikuyu instead of English, he revises significantly the political agenda of the African writer. Ngugi may not have succeeded in getting many writers to follow him: but his achievement may be in the undoubted fact that those who have questioned socio-economic dependence but not linguistic colonialism can, after his discussion of the politics of language, be no longer at ease.

NOTES

1. Ngugi Wa Thiong'o, *Decolonising the Mind* (London: James Currey, 1986), p. 160.
2. For a more detailed discussion on the introduction of English in India, see Tejaswini Niranjana's, "Translation, Colonialism and the Rise of English," *Economic and Political Weekly*, 25, No. 15 (1990), pp. 773-79 and Gauri Viswanathan's "The Beginnings of English Literary Studies in India," *Oxford Literary Review*, 9, No.1-2 (1989), pp. 2-27.
3. Ngugi Wa Thiong'o, "Return to the Roots," *Writers in Politics* (London: Heinemann, 1981), pp. 53-65.
4. Chinua Achebe, "Thoughts on the African Novel," *Hopes and Impediments* (1987; rpt. New York: Doubleday, 1989), p. 93.
5. Ngugi Wa Thiong'o, *Decolonising the Mind,* p. 21.
6. Amos Tutuola, *The Palm Wine Drinkard* (London: Faber and Faber, 1952), p. 6.
7. Edward W. Said, "Intellectuals in the Post-Colonial World," *Salmagundi*, 70-71 (1986), pp. 44-64.

Writers in Politics: Ngugi's *Detained* and KVR's *Detenu Diary*: A Study

N. SOMASEKHARA SARMA

Most writers of the third world countries who propose solutions to the problems of the society in putting an end to exploitative social relationship invariably found themselves in prison. This paper is an attempt to study the memoirs of two such writers, Ngugi of Kenya and KVR of Andhra Pradesh. While Ngugi is a novelist, KVR is a poet and critic. Both relentlessly fight against what they call neo/semi colonial culture imposed by the ruling classes.

Ngugi and KVR are primarily college teachers by profession, writers by vocation and Marxists in their outlook. They call their governments not independent but neo-colonial. Both propose armed revolution as the only way to pull down this exploitative structure. Of course they consider themselves soldiers of cultural army. And hence their fight against oppressive culture by propagating people's culture through their writings and speeches. Both are founder members of literary cultural organisations, Ngugi: Kamiruthu Community Education and Cultural Centre and KVR: A.P. Revolutionary Writers' Association. And of course both the organisations suffered the wrath of their governments, soon after their inception. If Kenyan government banned the staging of the play *Ngaahika Ndeenda* of KCECC, the A.P. Government proscribed two publications of A.P.R.W.A. *Jhanjha* and *Ippudu Veesthunna Gali*.

Both Ngugi and KVR feel that it is the bounden duty of a writer to support and propagate the cause of the downtrodden and the exploited. Ngugi professes his faith thus: "The writer as a human being is himself a product of history, of time and place. As a member of society he belongs to a certain class and he is inevitably a participant in the class struggle of his time."[1] KVR in his letter to Sri Sri says that their politics is to depict people's struggles in the light of revolutionary ideology. Nikhileswar, another revolutionary writer of A.P., asserts that they are committed writers and support revolution even if they don't have any link with any revolutionary party. Furthermore, Ngugi and KVR are inspired by armed peasants uprisings, Ngugi by Mau, Mau in Kenya, and KVR by the Naxalbari and Srikakulam armed struggles. No wonder all their writings reflected the people's struggle in a positive light, propagating anti-imperial and anti-feudal revolutions.

Thus their commitment to people's cause and their constant and incessant progapanda for a revolution through their writings have incensed their governments and resulted in their arrests. But they are undeterred by their arrests and their resolve to continue the fignt against what they call comprador bourgeoisie rule both in Kenya and India is revealed in their prison diaries. A close study of their prison diaries reveals a few similarities and also marked differences of the treatment of political detenus in the prisons of the independent Kenya and India.

Ngugi was arrested, rather abducted from his house, on the night of 30th December 1977. The Kenyatta government charged Ngugi with inciting class struggle in his play *Ngaahika Ndeenda*. But Ngugi asserts, rightly, that "*Ngaahika Ndeenda* did not invent classes in Kenya. Classes and class struggles have been the central facts of Kenyan history for the last eighty seven years." (188) He considers his imprisonment and the banning of the play as an onslaught on people's culture. Commenting on the futile but hideous attempts of the government to hide the realities of society Ngugi says, "Some people, it seems would rather smash the mirror that may show them the warts on their faces and then sit back with a smile of relief, saying 'thank God. I now have no warts.'" (175) Similar attempts by the A.P. Government drew similar remarks from Dr. P. Varavara Rao, a revolutionary writer. When the A.P. Govt. proscribed books published by Virasam, he challenged, "you can proscribe books which pronounce truth, but what can you do with the world which bears witness to it."

Ngugi and KVR, both being Marxists, consider their detention not as an individual affair, but a part of comprador bourgeoisie's attempt to crush people's struggle against colonial culture. Their faith that they are part of the long history of people's struggles against colonial and neo/semi colonial rule gives them the much-needed confidence to sustain their morale during their detention.

II

Ngugi's *Detained* consists of two sections: the first containing his experiences and reactions to various incidents in jail and his letters from prison, the second revealing the collusion between the government and the university authorities to deny him employment after his release. Ngugi's prison diary reveals his deep insight into the workings of the 'state' and his knowledge of Kenya's history and his Marxist understanding of the forces that propel changes. As a Marxist intellectual, he analyses how the colonial culture is sustained and abetted by the political power in the hands of ruling comprador bourgeoisies even after the so-called 'Independence.' For him culture is not an abstract thing, unlinked with economic relations. He says, "cultural domination is precisely a result and reflection of economic and political domination." (xv) He argues that colonial culture is an instrument in the hands of the ruling class to perpetuate their hegemony. It is "the culture of an oppressing minority desperately trying to impose total silence on a restive majority." (31) Its goal is to create an atmosphere of subservience in the society. The ruling class, to impose such culture, resort to "reactionary violence" on the toiling masses. A part of it is "detention without trial." As against this, Ngugi tried to propagate revolutionary culture "of courage, not fear, defiance to oppression, not submission; pride in oneself and in one's country, not cowardly acceptance of national humiliation." (66) To that effect he started a cultural organisation, KCECC, and prepared a script of *Ngaahika Ndeenda*, in Gikuyu. But the involvement of peasantry and its message of anti-colonial struggles created tremors in the Kenyatta government and the result was its ban. The play is an experiment of Mao's theory on art, "from people to people."

Ngugi's narration of the past history of Kenyan people's anti-colonial struggles reinforces his resolve to continue the struggle. The feeling that he is not alone in that struggle gives him the much-needed moral strength in his solitary confinement. Right from Waiyaki in 1890, to Mau Mau armed peasant uprising in 1956, to Ngugi, the history of Kenya is a saga of sacrifices for "real freedom." The "Uhuru," 1963, proved futile to the majority of Kenyans as the colonialist regime was replaced by their agents, comprador bourgeoisie class. Ngugi explains the nature of comprador bourgieosie; "Comprador bourgeoisie, but its very economic base, a dependent class, a parasite class. . . . It is in essence . . . a handsomely paid supervisor for the smooth operation of foreign economic interests. Its political inspiration and guidance come from outside the country." (56) That is why the toiling millions of Kenya find no change even after independence. KANU government is more ruthless and systematic in its suppression of people's movements and democratic rights. Ngugi calls the KANU,Comprador bourgeoisie government, a pimp that mortgaged the national interests. The same sentiment is expressed by Cherabanda Raju, a revolutionary poet of A.P., in his most popular and controversial poem in which he cried in anguish and anger, "Oh Mother! your beauty is such that every limb of yours is mortgaged in the international market."

If we look at the structure of Ngugi's prison diary, we find that his memoirs are not written in a chronological order. We can as well call it Ngugi's musings. Ngugi feels that many of the intellectuals are devoid of social commitment and are opportunistic. He attacks them for their tongue-in-cheek attitude towards people's movements. They talk progressive but act conservative. It is this opportunistic attitude of the Kenyan intellectuals that makes some political detenus wish that they are imprisoned so that they wake up to social reality. Intellectuals like Ngugi were very few who stood by the people. That was why Ngugi had to revive all his mental strength to sustain his faith in revolution during his solitary confinement. Any form of protest in jail, a whisper, a word of defiance etc., is the prisoner's self-assertion against suppression. Ngugi was kept alone and not allowed even to get books from outside. So he expresses his defiance by writing a novel surreptitiously in Gikuyu language. Of course, as a writer he needs people around him to write a novel. According to him, "A writer just takes down notes dictated to him by life among the people, which he then arranges in this or that form. I need life to write about life." (8-9) But in prison this lack of life was compensated for, sometimes by conversation between the prisoners, talks of sympathetic warders etc. He feels that the constant watch of the warders, while he was awake or asleep, is most unnerving. It was cruel human isolation created by the government to make him reconsider his resolve to continue his fight against the repressive culture of neo-colonialism. The prisoners were put on the tenterhooks of impending release or death that turned many prisoners into valium addicts. Any news from outside or rumour of their release was easily believed. However, Ngugi feels it is the inner strength of the prisoner and his faith in the correctness of his ideology that finally sustain his morale. "Resistance is only means of resisting a breakdown." (8-9) Ngugi was so firm in his resolve to fight any form of subservience to authorities, that he refused to wear chains, and thus missed medical aid and a rare interview with his wife and children. As he says, "it was the expectation and requirement of detainee's cooperation in his slavery that I found more repugnant." (27) He never regrets his decision to propagate people's culture. Moreover, he feels sorry for he wasted many years in serving the colonial culture and language. "To write for, to speak for and work for the lives of peasants and workers was the highest call of patriotic duty." (105) This single statement is enough to reveal Ngugi's commitment to people. Ngugi resolves, "I have accepted the lot of all writers who try to hold clear mirror into the motions of human thought, human society and history in general."(191) But he knows that he is not a lone literary soldier, for he says, "We, who write in Kenya, in Africa, in the third world, are modern Cassandras of the developing world, condemned to cry the truth against neo-colonialists and imperialist cultures and then be ready to pay for it with incarceration, exile and even death." (191)

Ngugi's observation proves right even in regard to the A.P. Revolutionary writers in India. Some of them lost their jobs, and a few died a martyr's death and of course many of them were jailed for their commitment to the people's cause and KVR's diary mirrors the anti-democratic nature of successive Andhra Pradesh governments.

KVR's *Detenu Diary* reveals his computer-like recording of his day-to-day reactions, comments on the happenings both inside and outside prison and his interaction with his colleagues. While Ngugi missed the intellectual company, KVR had the opportunity of staying with some of the members of his organisation (A.P.R.W.A.). As every dark cloud has its silver lining, so also Ngugi's loneliness saved him from the mortal fears of the disintegration of his organisation and from being a silent observer of the meek surrender of some of his colleagues. KVR had to pass through that agony. But his only solace was that he was not a lone fighter among the prisoners but he had the company of his colleagues Varavara Rao, Madhusudhana Rao, Cherabanda Raju, to mention a few. However the activities of Sri Sri, the founder president of A.P.R.W.A., and the resignation of R.V. Sastry, a noted novelist, had their own impact on KVR. In a mood of self-abnegation he was critical of himself, "Suffer I must, suffer I will, if suffering is the only reward at least of the half baked and half settled political opinion of mine."[2] This mood of depression raised doubts about the rightness of the revolutionary path. KVR discovered petty bourgeoisie's romantic heroism in the activities of the Naxalite movement. But his self-depreciation and wavering were the class nature of KVR and his ilk who were in the process of declassing themselves. The petty bourgeoisie's vacillating nature dominates when the revolutionary movements are in crises. Apart from it, his sentimental and emotional attachment to his organisation, given his fear of seeing its disintegration even as he was its secretary, led KVR to that thinking. This kind of vacillation we don't find in Ngugi, for he rose from the family of peasants which had already sacrificed one son to the people's cause.

The reactions of Ngugi and KVR differ as much as they appear similar, in spite of their similar world outlook. Ngugi was primarily a novelist who did not have long history of involvement in or attachment to any people's movement. KVR had been a cultural activist for almost two decades then and he was actively involved in progressive literary movements. Hence we find more intensity in the sentiments expressed by KVR and also more subjective elements in his diary. Ngugi had to rely on the long history of Kenya's anti-colonial struggle to get inspiration, while KVR has the contemporary revolutionary movement to boost his morale. Ngugi's ire is directed against Western imperialism, whereas KVR attacks Soviet Social Imperialism along with American Imperialism. KVR's knowledge of world affairs is deep and his analysis of the Indian political scene is wider for he had an opportunity, even in detention, to read newspapers and books. As Ngugi accuses Kenyatta believing the hopes of the Kenyans, KVR is bitter of both the ruling pro-Soviet regime and the pro-American opposition. Their analysis of the class nature of their rulers reveals their Marxist understanding.

It is not irrelevant here to say that the prison conditions in A.P. are not as severe as those in Kenya, comparatively. KVR was permitted to get books from outside and read newspapers even if some items were censored. He had ample leisure and opportunity to discuss with his colleagues. He was not denied white paper unlike Ngugi who had to write his novel on toilet paper. Ngugi had to rely on his memory to narrate Kenyan history. KVR had read almost 40 books, took notes from them and also scribbled some reviews. He was busy not only with books, writing poetry, discussing with friends but also settling issues concerning his organisation. Ngugi was deprived of all these facilities (if these can be called facilities) and his diary does not contain much information about the activities of cultural organisations in Kenya. If Ngugi's comments were limited to politics and culture, there is no field that is not touched by KVR, political, economic, literary and even personal affairs of the fellow prisoners. This comparative study of prison conditions may lead some of the readers to the opinion that after all the Indian ruling class is more liberal towards political detenus. But if we read those prison conditions in their historical background, we learn that it is the people's struggles against fascist regime that relaxed its grip.

But whatever may be the difference in the treatment and approach of Ngugi and KVR, their prison memoirs reveal that the comprador bourgeoisie ruling classes in these countries do not tolerate any kind of opposition to their rule; they are more ruthless and brutal than their colonial masters. If such is the negative side of the picture we get from the prison diaries, the positive side is that we have writers in the third world countries who are ready to sacrifice their personal comforts, and sometimes even their lives, in their fight against repressive regimes.

NOTES

1. Ngugi, *Detained: A Writer's Prison Diary* (London: Heinemann, 1981, rpt. 1987), p. 72. All subsequent citations are from this edition.
2. K.V. Ramana Reddy, *Detenu Diary* (Telugu) (Kavali, Andhra Pradesh, India: Jhujha, undated), p. 166. All citations are from this edition.

The Writer's Conscience: A Reading of Nadine Gordimer's *The Essential Gesture*

C. SUBBARAO

To be "only a writer" or to be "more than a writer," is the question which has acquired an urgency and relevance in South Africa, the like of which is rarely raised anywhere else. The subject of Nadine Gordimer's *The Essential Gesture* (Penguin 1989) is just this question which seems to generate an unresolvable conflict in the mind of the writer (more in the case of the white South African writer). I wish to take the Gordimer essay as a point of departure for an examination of some issues related to a writer's social responsibility and a writer's creative commitment to his craft.

I use the phrase 'Writer's Conscience' as an evaluative concept. When I hear that Gordimer is referred to as the voice of conscience of South Africa, I feel a little more encouraged to use the phrase. Moreover, I would like to make a distinction between consciousness and conscience. What I would like to do is to study the manner in which writers embody their awareness of the injustice and suffering in the world. In what manner do they respond to it? In what kind of style do they embody this experience? Does the treatment reflect only an awareness? Or does it enable the reader to move beyond mere reading and does it move the reader finally to action? These are some of the distinctions I try to make in using the terms, conciousness and conscience. We come across occasionally a kind of writer whose exploration of the miseries of the world is so powerful that we sense a conscience behind the treatment, not merely an awareness of the problem.

What do we mean then by referring to the conscience of the writer? Do we expect him to take sides and declare himself? Are we not asking him to be "more than a writer"?

We are all aware of the charge levelled against the clerisy by Julian Benda. He talked of the "Treason of the Clerks." The intellectual who ought to know and who is also aware of what is to be done, sometimes refuses to move or be moved. Action is anathema to him. He is content to contemplate. No wonder people like Benda consider mere contemplation as an indulgence. In Tikkana's version of the *Mahabharata* episode about the assault on Draupadi in the court, he makes use of a phrase "Upeksha," indifference. When the system is corrupted, and if the "sresthas," the best men in society, indulge in 'Upeksha,' it will be to their detriment. Was it not Yeats who said:

> Things fall apart: the centre cannot hold; . . .
> The best lack all conviction, while the worst
> Are full of passionate intensity.

Tikkana manages to take shelter under a divine dispensation which for him would finally bring about order and cleanse the system. If you do not believe in a divine dispensation, there is recourse to irony as could be seen in Shakespeare:

> Lilies that fester smell far worse than weeds.

The predicament of the writer in the third world is whether to be "only a writer" or to be "more than a writer." How does he balance the two claims? Would he withstand the pressure of the double demand and yet make meaning?

Gordimer quotes approvingly of Barthes from whom the title of the essay is taken:

> A writer's work is his essential gesture as a social being.

According to Gordimer, in South Africa a double demand is placed on the writer. The social significance of the writer is emphasised. The writer has to act as a spokesperson for the oppressed. And in the process, he invites on himself punishment from the state. The writer's "Essential Gesture" as a social being involves taking risks. In the case of the South African writer the essential gesture by which he enters the brotherhood of man is the revolutionary gesture:

> It is from the moment when I shall no longer be more than a writer that I shall cease to write.
>
> Camus

The question that Gordimer wants to consider is this: what right has the society to impose responsibility upon writers and what right has the writer to resist? She would like to examine not what is *forbidden* by the state or censorship but "to what we are *bidden* as writers." What is expected of the writer by the dynamic of collective conscience, as she could see? A greater value is sought to be placed on the *persona* outside of the writer. No value is given if one is no more than a writer. A writer's greatness is measured in terms of the responsibility to society that he accepts. The writer's responsibility to art, to his craft of writing as such, is not held superior to his responsibility to society and to the people at large.

Gordimer recognises the society's right to make demands on the writer even as she considers it equal to that of the writer's commitment to his artistic vision. If society has a right to demand certain things from the writer, the writer also has a right to affirm his allegiance to art. His integrity as human being and writer is in direct proportion to his ability to balance the conflict and bring about harmony.

Gordimer refers to *two* kinds of writers: "those for whom writing is a revolutionary activity no different from and to be practised concurrently with running a political trade union, and those who interpret their society's demand to be more than a writer as something that may yet be fulfilled through the nature of their writing itself."

Is the predicament of the South African white writer unique? Can we cite instances of the conflict between creativity and responsibility from other cultures and other countries? Perhaps it is not unique. There have always been writers whose intergrity as human beings is shown to be in conflict with the integrity of the writer as writer. Only the problem acquires a special urgency in the case of the African writer:

> His integrity as a human being demands the sacrifice of everything to the struggle put up on the side of free man. His integrity as a writer goes the moment he begins to write what he is told he ought to write. (*A Writer's Freedom*, 1975, 106)

In Gordimer's strikingly paradoxical phrase, "To gain his freedom the writer must give up his freedom." The Black South African writer submits to an unwritten orthodoxy of interpretation and representation in his work. He gives up his freedom, "his private emotions," in order to prove his blackness as a revolutionary condition. But not all black writers could agree to this loss of freedom and to the assumption of revolutionary responsibility as orthodoxy. They have begun to negotiate the right to their own, inner interpretation of the essential gesture by which they are part of the black struggle.

If this is the predicament of the aware black writer, the conflicts faced by the white writer are much worse. The responsibility of raising the threshold of the consciousness of the white people is his task as "cultural worker." In declaring himself on the side of black freedom struggle, the white writer accepts a political responsibility, if not an actual orthodoxy.

> Writers in South Africa who are 'only writers' are sometimes reproached by those, black and white, who are in practical revolutionary terms 'more than writers,' for writ-

> ing of events as if they themselves had been at the heart of action, endurance and suffering. So far as black writers are concerned, even though the humiliations and deprivations of daily life under apartheid enjoin them, many of them were no more among the children under fire from the police in the seventies, or are among the students and miners shot, tear-gassed and beaten in the eighties, or are living as freedom fighters in the bush, than Akhmatova was a heart-broken wife or mother separated from a son she had nurtured. Given these circumstances, their claim to generalise and speak for a human predicament in extremity comes from the lesser or greater extent of their ABILITY to do so; and the development of that ability is their responsibility towards those with whom they are united by this extrapolation of suffering and resistance. White writers who are 'only writers' are open to related reproach for 'stealing the lives of blacks' as good material. Their claim to this 'material' is the same as the black writers' at an important existential remove nobody would discount. Their essential gesture can be fulfilled only in the integrity Chekhov demanded: 'to describe a situation so truthfully . . . that the reader can no longer evade it.' (*The Essential Gesture,* 299)

Instances can be cited where the double demand that Gordimer refers to, far from generating friction or conflict, acts as a creative catalyst to bring about harmony and the desired result. I refer here to the example of Vaclav Havel, the Czech President, once a prisoner of conscience and now the philosopher-king. It is Havel who develops this idea of individual conscience and the concept of the 'Power of the Powerless,' the power of the common man whose individual conscience becomes the Archimedian point from which Havel would move the earth, as it were. And move he did, literally in 1989 when the collective conscience of the people is enabled to discover not only its power, but more importantly, its identity. It is a rare instance of a writer whose commitment to his people and to his writing is seen and shown to be one and the same. He is at once a writer and more than a writer.

We have instances in our own literature, in our vernacular, where a writer is seen fulfilling his role, at once, as writer and as more than writer. We have the instance of the poet, singer, activist and revolutionary who goes by the name of Gaddar. What better example can one offer than this phenomenon of a poet whose songs represent the suffering and the misery of the common man while showing a way out, a break through? I cannot recall a similar instance of a poet who is at one with his craft and vocation. There is no dichotomy whatsoever in the case of Havel and the form and content of Gaddar's work as also his theory and practice. We must grant that not all can follow the example of either Havel or Gaddar. A number of writers occupy a middle ground whose passion and perception, feeling and form closely resemble the work of Gaddar.

If authenticity is understood as reconciliation of the conflict between external obligation/demand and internal impulse/experience, examples of Soyinka, Achebe or Vaclav Havel, Milan Kundera or Sri Sri or Gaddar can be cited. In the creative union of external motion and internal emotion, the authentic voice of the writer's conscience/his essential gesture can be identified.

In the final analysis, Gordimer urges the conclusion that a writer is basically one who transforms experience. As she herself puts it: "The transformation of experience remains the writer's essential gesture; the lifting out of a limited category something that reveals its full meaning and significance only when the writer's imagination has expanded it."

Isn't Gordimer suggesting that in order to be "more than a writer," one has to be necessarily "more of a writer"?

INDEX

Achebe, Chinua 13-15, 16, 17, 18, 19n, 20n, 48-49, 57n, 58n, 59, **66-70, 71-78, 79-86,** 99-100, 118
African Literature as Restoration of Celebration" 48-49, 58n
Aluko, T.M. 17, 19n
Anthills of the Savannah 13-15, 19n
Armah, Ayi Kwei **59-65**
Arnold, Matthew 16
Arrow of God 17, 20n, 69, 73, 74, 75, 76, 77, 78n
Awoonor, Kofi 59

Bacchae of Euripides, The 21, 24-25, **26-27**, 31n, **41-46**
Beautyful Ones are Not Yet Born, The 59, 60
Black Skins, White Masks 95n
Bound to Violence 59

Camus, Albert 115
Caitaani Mutharabaini 102
Clark, J.P. **47-58**
Cocteau 22

Dance of the Forest, A 26
Daniel Deronda 13
Detained: A Writer's Prison Diary 96n, **105-12**
Detenu Diary **105-12**
Devil on the Cross 102
Dinesen, Isaak 90
Dorrit 13

Echewa, T. Obinkaram 16, 19n
Eliot, George 79
Eliot, T.S. 23, 24, 31n
Essential Gesture, The **113-18**
Euripides **41-46**

Fables of Identity 37, 40n
Facing Mount Kenya 87
Fanon, Frantz 87, 95n, 99
Flaubert, Gustav 13
Four Quartets 23
Fragments 60
Frye, Northrop 37, 40n

Gordimer, Nadine **113-18**
Grain of Wheat, A 87, 88, 94
Greene, Graham 15

Havel, Vaclav 118
Healers, The 59-65
Homecoming 87
Huxley, Elspeth 90

Idanre 16, 21 **33-40**
Idea of a Christian Society, The 24, 31n
"Image of Africa," An 57n
Interpreters, The 19, 28, 32n, 59
Ippudv Vesthunna Gali 105

James, Henry 13
Jhanja 105

Kenyatta, Jomo 87
King John **16-17**
Kundera, Milan 118

Land's Lord 17, 19n, 20n
"Language of African Literature," The 89-90, 96n
Lawrence, D.H. 13
Laye, Camara 59
Lion and the Jewel 30

Madmen and Specialists 21, **24-26**, 31n
Mahabharata, The 114
Man Died, The 21, 22, 29, 31n
Man of the People, A 75-76, 80, **82-85**, 86n
Masquerade 49
Middlemarch 79
Mimic Men, The 83, 86n
Morning Yet on Creation Day 70
Mugo, Micere 87
Murder in the Cathedral 26, 31n
Myth, Literature and the African World 16, 33, 40n

Naipaul, V.S. 83, 86n
No Longer at Ease 72, 76
Ngaahika Ndeena 102, 105, 106, 108
Ngugi Wa Thiong'o 59, **87-97**, **98-104**, **105-12**
Nikhileswar 106

Okara, Gabriel 59
One Man, One Wife 17, 19n
Opera Wonyosi 30
Orphee Negree 23
Ouologuem, Yambo 59
Ozidi **47-58**

Palm Wine Drinkard, The 100, 104n
Petals of Blood 59, 88, 96n
Play of the Giants, A 30
Primitive Religion 21

Radiance of the King, The 59
Radin, Paul 21
Raft, The 49
Raju, Cherabanda 108
Rao, P. Varavara 107
Reddy, K.V. Ramana **105-12**
Reed in the Time, A 47
Requiem for a Futurologist 30
"Return to the Roots" 99
River Between, The 87, 88, 93

Season of Anomy 21, **22-24**, 28, 31n, 32n
Shakespeare, William 114
Shuttle in the Crypt 21, 22, 29, 30, 31n, 32n
Song of a Goat 49, 53, 58n
Soyinka, Wole 16, 19, **21-32**, **33-40**, 48, 49, 59, 118
Sri, Sri 106, 118

Things Fall Apart 18, **66-70**, 73, 76, 77, 78n, **80-82**, 85n, 86n
This Earth, My Brother 59
"Thoughts on the African Novel" 99, 104n
Trial of Dedan Kimathi, The 87, 88, 95
Tutuola, Amis 87, 100, 104n
Two Thousand Seasons 60

Voice, The 59

Waste Land, The 23, 24
Weep Not, Child 87, 88, 94-95, 96n
Whitman, Walt 15
Why are we so Blest? 60
Wretched of the Earth, The 95n

Yeats, W.B. 114